Common Core And The Truth

A Parent's Journey into the Heart of the Core

Amy Skalicky

Forward by:
Kris Nielsen

Table of Contents

Forward

One of the biggest selling points of the Common Core State Standards Initiative was that it would create opportunities for students to become critical thinkers in preparation for the 21st-Century knowledge economy. There are a couple of problems with that claim. First, teachers have been learning and sharing best practices for this task in their own local and professional communities for quite some time, without the outside help of non-educators. Second, there is no explicit critical thinking framework within in the Common Core Standards. (Close reading and primary documents are the tools that reformers claim to lead to critical thinking, which means that they are not real keen on the meaning of the term.)

Thankfully, there is one very powerful group of people who have been exercising real critical thinking, and they've been using it to figure out what's behind the talking points and beatitudes of education reform. Moms and dads are catching on, and they are asking harder and harder questions. They're sharing sources and checking them against others. This is probably not what the authors and framers and funders behind the Common Core Standards had in mind.

In this book, Amy Skalicky takes us through her journey as a critical mom; a mom that dives into the rabbit hole of education reform and uncovers more than she thought was possible. Amy also shares how this has transformed her from frightened to determined. It's a transition that seems to happen rather quickly for parents defending their children from threat. Education reform, as it's happening right now, is the most important and real threat to our kids.

I've spent the better part of three years learning about the Common Core Standards and the bigger picture around them. It's been surreal, frightening, and angering. Thanks to parents like

Amy Skalicky, it's starting to look better, as more and more parents and citizens are awaken and moved to act against a monstrosity that has not yet settled into place. We still have time to change this, to beat it, and fix it. It will take education from each other and from parents like Amy.

Amy delved into everything she's learned so far, and offers more than enough resources for her readers to follow up. Her journey into learning more about the Common Core has opened other doors that prompted her to do further research. Some may find that her material veers off from the initiative or the standards themselves, but as she states in her introduction, she hopes that this will be a way for parents and concerned citizens to find out what's happening all around us and our kids, and will prompt further discussion and learning.

Kris Nielsen

Author and Education Advocate

Introduction

I first heard about Common Core almost a year ago. I was looking at Christmas candy at Walmart and, as customary, I struck up a conversation with another mom close by. During the conversation, I learned that she was a homeschool mom, and that she was fearful of something called Common Core. I asked if she could elaborate, and I got the rundown there in the seasonal isle of the store. I left with my head buzzing, thinking maybe she was a little crazy and even exaggerating just a bit. I was aware there was an effort to standardize some things, but the snippets of information I had heard (funny how the media was very quiet about this for a long time) didn't sound threatening or even that big of a deal. There was no way that what she shared could possibly be true, not in America, anyway.

I was wrong.

Incredibly, head-in-the-sand, on cruise-control-in-my-own-comfort-zone kind of wrong. Common Core is not just another education reform movement. Common Core is completely different, and very, very ugly. I did not want to believe any of it, as most of us don't, but deafening my ears in denial because I did not want to deal with it was not going to make it go away. As I absorbed the enormity of the information I was gathering, I realized that I was shocked, saddened, angered and terrified of what I read. As I engaged in conversations with parents and teachers across the country, I discovered that my feelings were not unique. This is America! How could this possibly be happening? Then it all began to sink in, and I realized just how pervasive our government had become, and how long they had been at it, causing the pit in my stomach to grow into a sickening ball of fear.

I am a parent, like many of you reading this book. My son is an adult now, almost 22, and still trying to figure out what he wants to do "when he grows up," which is fine. He's free to find his way, as we all did in one way or another. My daughter, Miki, is nine-years-old, in the fourth grade, and full of life. She is gifted, a terrific questioner and thinker, and loves learning like nobody's business. Her favorite subjects have always been math, science and writing. Miki currently has about 15 different things on her "What I Want to Be When I Grow Up" list, and I will do everything possible to ensure she has the opportunity to explore every one of them. I pray that she has the opportunity to discover her own way and cultivate the gifts God has bestowed upon her. I nurture and protect these qualities as I am raising her, as I did with my son, and encourage them both to be the best versions of who they are—loving, honest, hardworking, compassionate, inquisitive, literate, and careful. I pray for space to grow and blossom. I also model and teach values and character, grounded in the Bible. This is not only my responsibility as a parent, it is also my right, and there is a good book called the Bible, a Constitution, federal laws, a world history and common sense that supports this. No matter what your personal beliefs are, this is our right as parents.

Let me take you back in time for a moment, the time before the attacks of September 11, 2011 occurred. Do you remember America then? We were the bravest, the strongest, the smartest—the people that everyone wanted to be and the country everyone wanted to live. Nobody could every hurt us, for if they so much as grumbled in our direction, we'd give 'em the boot in the butt, right? None of the craziness we saw happening in other parts of the world could ever happen here. We were America, and nobody could touch us.

Until they did.

We are facing a similar catastrophe with Common Core. I've heard the comments: "No, it can't possibly be that bad." What's wrong with national standards?" Our kids can't read or write, we have to do something." Even "The government said this is what Common Core is…you are just a conspiracy theorist and way out there." I did not want to believe any of this either; I dug through reliable sources of information, thinking at first that I was only hearing about the extreme situations, that Common Core had to be perfectly reasonable and that everything would be fine.

I was wrong again.

Everything in this book is carefully researched. I would have liked to have ventured deeper into a number of topics presented here, but time and space only allow for so much. I chose historical information as well as details and documentation of current events to draw a decisive picture of what we are faced with. Some topics are highly contentious, and I assure you that I share information for the sake of parents becoming more informed and not to pick on any one person or group. Common Core is a problem for all of us, regardless of party affiliation, religion, sexual orientation, race, economic status and beliefs. It hurts homeschoolers, private schools, parochial schools and public schools. While it is easy to find ourselves at odds with one another because of our differences, we must realize that Common Core hurts all children, punishes all teachers, and tramples the rights of all parents. It is time to put aside our differences and unite. Parents and educators, as well as schools and district administration, are all faced with Common Core and we must work together to fight it.

Common Core is happening right now, and new developments surface almost daily, so it is important to understand the most recent information available. I urge you to read this book, and then dig even deeper. What I share with you here is the tip of the ice berg. It is everywhere, even in the Girl Scouts. Yes, the Girl Scouts of America is aligned with Common Core (Skalicky 2013). There are several other excellent books I recommend as well, such as Kris Nielsen's Children of the Core and Uncommon, Charlotte Iserbyt's The Deliberate Dumbing Down of American, Professor Christopher Tienken's The School Reform Landscape and anything by Dianne Ravitch, for they all present additional information based on different expertise—all essential to thoroughly absorb Common Core's gravity.

The Common Core Standards Initiative has taken everything I've experienced as an American and shaken it to the core, so to speak. Freedom, rights, the Constitution, parenting, Christianity, leadership, government, trust—many things look very different now, and some I don't even recognize anymore.

But, I am no longer frightened. I am determined. You see, I still believe in that Good Book, that Constitution, those laws (the legally-enacted ones, anyway) and the lessons taught by history. I believe there are more Americans who do care about our children than don't. There is much work to be done, and it's not going to be easy. I am a fighter, and I pray that you are too.

Say "Hello" to the Common Core Standards Initiative

"You can't make socialists out of individualists—children who know how to think for themselves spoil the harmony of the collective society, which is coming, where everyone is interdependent."

–John Dewey

Here is what the official Common Core Standards Initiative website says in its mission statement: "The Common Core State Standards provide a consistent, clear understanding of what students are expected to learn, so teachers and parents know what they need to do to help them. The standards are designed to be robust and relevant to the real world, reflecting the knowledge and skills that our young people need for success in college and careers. With American students fully prepared for the future, our communities will be best positioned to compete successfully in the global economy (Achieve 2012)." Further, the standards are designed to enhance "rigor" and are "evidence-based" and claim that they do not tell teachers how to teach or what to teach.

In the Frequently Asked Questions section of the website, it states this: *"The Common Core State Standards Initiative is a state-led effort that established a single set of clear educational standards for kindergarten through 12th grade in English language arts and mathematics that states voluntarily adopt. The standards are designed to ensure that students graduating from high school are prepared to enter credit bearing entry courses in two or four year college programs or enter the workforce. The standards are clear and concise to ensure that parents, teachers, and students have a clear understanding of the expectations in reading, writing, speaking and listening, language and mathematics in school* (Achieve 2012)."

Sounds like a worthwhile endeavor, right? What parent doesn't want a better education for their child? Parents share similar goals of raising children to become successful adults according to how they define success, as well as be prepared to enter the workforce with good paying jobs. Parents hope that their children pursue interests that they enjoy, develop belief systems and habits that are healthy and reflect the values parents choose to teach them, and choose careers that meet their needs, and those of their families should they choose. I intentionally used the words "choose" and "choice" to emphasize the importance of that right. The right of parents, and as appropriate, their children, to make choices and decisions is a critical component of the Common Core Standards Initiative.

I want to lay a bit of groundwork before I go any deeper into Common Core itself. I want to talk about the use of language, words that sell, and relativism, the creation of gray areas to weaken absolute beliefs. The government and corporate creators of the standards use the same carefully chosen key words and phrases to sell the Common Core Standards Initiative.

Think, for a moment, about the advertisements that we are bombarded with almost every day. What is their purpose? The goal is to get you to buy something, right? Think about the extensive sales psychology research that is conducted on consumers and their habits. The federal government does no less, and they have become the sleaziest used-car salesmen on the lot.

The government and corporate players use ambiguous terminology that requires capable detective skills to dissect and uncover the true meaning of almost every word. Understanding this is imperative to understanding what the government and corporations are trying to accomplish. Make no mistake about it— large corporations are leading policy decisions in our government, and education is no exception. While I am not going to lead us into a debate about political systems, I am going to point out here that a hallmark of Marxism is government by corporation. I will, however, talk more about corporate involvement later in the book.

Common Core plays with language to sell people. "Creative, deep learning, collaboration and analytical work" that the author states teachers want, is subject to the federal government's interpretation, meaning that creative is find as long as it remains within the boundaries it sets, deep learning based on ridiculous, non-evidence based attempts at establishing 'rigor,' collaboration meaning socialist robots, and analytical work is the ever present 'how did you arrive at your answer' to the 1st grader on an addition problem convoluted by 'new math'" (Achieve 2012)

Common Core likes the phrase "rich data." The word "rich" has always had a yummy sound to it—rich chocolate, rich colors, rich leather—creates a sensation of being awesome, set apart, elite..."rich" is used to cloak a meaning, allowing it to get lost in the feelings it invokes. "Rich" in this context means extremely broad in scope, detailed, and private—no stone will be unturned. The perceptions one can easily get from hearing the justification for gathering "rich data" and what it will be used for might sound pretty good upfront—"specially designing products to meet individual needs" (Achieve 2012)—almost makes me feel like my daughter's education would be custom-designed just for her, except that it won't be. While it was initially claimed, and I can still find it on government, school and common core-affiliated websites, that the "rich data" would not go to a third party or, this information will not be shared or accessed, think again. It has already been admitted that the data collected will be sold to the highest bidder so they can develop products for a growing new market. I want to repeat that: **the data collected will be sold to the highest bidder so they can develop products for a growing new market.** Bill Gates later confirmed this by saying "...identifying common standards is just the starting point. We will only know if this effort has succeeded when the curriculum and tests are aligned to these standards ... When the tests are aligned to the common standards, the curriculum will line up as well, and it will unleash a powerful market of people providing services for better teaching" (Beck 2013) .

Read this line and think about it for a moment: "... (students will) be open and responsive to new and diverse perspectives; incorporate group input and feedback into the work" (Achieve 2012). These are some of the components of the development of 21st century skills as defined by the Partnership for 21st Century Skills, founded to complement and support the implementation of Common Core, and is a partnership with the US Department of Education (the federal government again) and various corporations such as Microsoft, Pearson, Ford Motor Company, the National Education Association, Crayola, and the National Board for Professional Teaching Standards (Skills 2002). Both of these concepts are salted throughout material written to promote Common Core. I certainly support teamwork and good skills to work together in a group, and I am a strong proponent of being open to new ideas. I want my daughter to be open to new ideas, and to have the skills to analyze each one thoughtfully before accepting or rejecting them. I value research and critical thinking skills; however, while the phrase "critical thinking skills" crops up often in pro-Common Core material, I don't see evidence of it. Strong critical thinking skills are characteristic of strong individuals, and Common Core does not seem to like that. In addition, teamwork does not mean always supporting a consensus. Sometimes the consensus is wrong, either factually, morally or ethically, or ideas are presented that infringe upon particular religious beliefs or are simply lacking in details, all of which are scenarios in which an individual needs to have the freedom and the skills, as well as the knowledge, to speak out. I do not know of any parents who want schools and government teaching our children what to think. What are teams and groups comprised of, and why are they not only sometimes desirable, but also often successful? Teams and groups consist of individuals with their own unique perspective, expertise, skills, knowledge base, strengths, weaknesses, ideas, creativity, experience and resources. Isn't that the beauty of the concept? I don't see the balance in Common Core that recognizes this value.

Below is Merriam-Webster's definition of rigor. Let me know if you see anything in there you would like applied to your child.

1. strictness, severity, or harshness, as in dealing with people.

2. the full or extreme severity of laws, rules, etc.

3. severity of living conditions; hardship; austerity: the rigor of wartime existence.

4. a severe or harsh act, circumstance, etc.

5. scrupulous or inflexible accuracy or adherence: the logical rigor of mathematics.

6. severity of weather or climate or an instance of this: the rigors of winter (Dictionary n.d.)

It is my hope that my daughter is sufficiently challenged throughout her education to encourage growth, exploration and learning. Rigor? Not so much. I am going to use the math standards as an example of this, as evidenced by this quote from a document called "What Does it Really Mean to Be College and Career Ready? The Mathematics and English Literacy Required of First Year Community College Students" developed by the National Center on Education and Economy: "It makes no sense to rush through the middle school mathematics curriculum in order to get to advanced algebra as rapidly as possible...Mastery of Algebra II is widely thought to be a prerequisite for success in college and careers. Our research shows that that is not so. The most demanding mathematics courses typically required of community college students are those required by the mathematics department, not the career major, but the content of the first year mathematics courses offered by the community colleges' mathematics department is typically the content usually associated with Algebra I, some Algebra II and a few topics in geometry. It cannot be the case that one must know Algebra II in order to study Algebra I or Algebra II. Based on our data, one cannot make the case that high school graduates must be proficient in Algebra II to be ready for college and careers... The high school mathematics curriculum is now centered on the teaching of a sequence of courses leading to calculus that includes Geometry, Algebra II, Pre-Calculus and Calculus...To require these courses in high school is to deny to many students the opportunity to graduate high school because they have not mastered a sequence of mathematics courses they will never need. In the face of these findings, the policy of requiring a passing score on an Algebra II exam for high school graduation simply cannot be justified... " (David T. Conley June) Notice the bold letters in the title of the paper. I will be talking more later about how the standards are actually focused on community college preparedness, not four-year university readiness. Their research? They have yet to produce it. However, there is plenty of research and evidence that makes it clear that the Common Core State Standard Initiative is not focused on providing our students with every opportunity possible to be the best that they can be and open doors to the future for them; on the contrary, it assumes that our students can only be mediocre, so they provide standards based on that assumption. Those who excel will be hand selected for special opportunities not available to the average student. So, on the one hand, we are talking robust, and on the other, we are diluting curriculum.

I am also going to talk more about the Common Core Standards Initiative and its relationship with the Workforce Investment Act. The one thing I want to point out now is that the

Common Core Standards are heavily designed for economic development, not education. Note that the phrase "smaller learning communities" is scattered throughout the Common Core documentation. "Smaller Learning Communities" are really "career clusters," or as the Career Technical Education website states, "The Career Clusters® and related Career Pathways serve as an organizing tool for schools, small learning communities, academies and magnet schools to develop more effective programs of study and curriculum" (Education 2013). The organization is "helping our nation meet the very real and immediate challenges of economic development, student achievement and global competitiveness," and further quotes from a report from Achieve about the Common Core Standards by saying the "…the CCSS are designed to cover most of the skills in greatest demand by employers, postsecondary systems and our society, including the ability of students to communicate effectively in a variety of ways, work collectively, think critically, solve routine and non-routine problems, and analyze information and data" (Achieve, Understanding the Skills of the Common Core Education Standards 2013). You can read more about the Career Technical Educational goals and how they informed the Common Core Standards on their website under the Career Clusters tab.

You will see other terms and phrases, such as "state led," "voluntary," "college and career ready," and "robust and relevant" throughout Common Core material that are hallmarks of the initiative. This is not by accident. A key principle in marketing is repetition. Not only is the choice of words important, but how many times your key phrases reach your audience is as well. Successful marketing strategies strive to create name or brand recognition, as well as concept recognition, and this technique is highly successful. Remember the saying "It's not what you say, but how you say it?" And, when all else fails, lie. Common Core has it all mastered.

Some marketing strategies are downright devious. For instance, the Common Core website and some publications about

Common Core go so far as to claim that the Common Core standards were written by a task force of education experts that included teachers, parents, content specialists and community experts, among others. One such description can be found in a booklet written for the state of Colorado entitled Understanding Common Core State Standards, written by John Kendall, who, according to the "About the Author" page at the end of the booklet "… is Senior Director in Research at Mid-continent Research for Education and Learning (McREL) in Denver, Colorado. Having joined McREL in 1988, Mr. Kendall conducts research and development activities related to academic standards. He directs a technical assistance unit that provides standards-related services to schools, districts, and states and to national and international organizations. He is the author of Content Knowledge: A Compendium of Standards and Benchmarks for K–12 Education and author or coauthor of numerous reports and guides related to standards-based systems, including High School Standards and Expectations for College and the Workplace; Essential Knowledge: The Debate Over What American Students Should Know; and Finding the Time to Learn: A Guide. A former Latin instructor, he holds an M.A. in Classics and a B.A. in English Language and Literature from the University of Colorado at Boulder." Here is what he has written on pages 1 and 2: "The Council of Chief State School Officers (CCSSO) and the National Governors Association (NGA) committed to this work with representatives from 48 states, 2 territories, and the District of Columbia. The task engaged the talents and expertise of educators, content specialists, researchers, community groups, and national organizations, including an advisory group of experts from Achieve, ACT, the College Board, the National Association of State Boards of Education, and the State Higher Education Executive Officers. The subject-area organizations, including the National Council of Teachers of English (NCTE) and the National Council of Teachers of Mathematics (NCTM), were not asked to help draft or provide feedback to early drafts of the standards but were invited to critique drafts of the Common Core standards prior to their release for public comment. In addition, the draft standards were informed by feedback from teachers, parents, business leaders, and the general public." (Kendall 2011). This claim has since been publicly been disproved. In other words, it's a lie. My only hope is that Mr. Kendall was told this and truly believed it, and did not intentionally set out to mislead readers.

Hold on, because we are just now getting started.

Venturing back in history for a moment, the national standardization movement took center stage with the No Child Left Behind Act (NCLB) of 2002 under George W. Bush. It was a bipartisan attempt to develop a set of K-12 standards in English, language arts, and math on a national basis that would better prepare students for coursework in college as well as post-college careers. It would fix our so-called broken schools. After all, to gain buy-in for changes, you have to convince people that what you want to change is broken in the first place. Diane Ravitch, former U.S. Assistant Secretary of Education under both the Clinton and Bush Administrations, observed at the time that the proposed writing of national educational standards by the CCSSO and NGA, the standards would be voluntary and would be a guideline, not a rigid structure to be strictly enforced, and certainly not mandatory to secure funding from the federal government (Ravitch 2010). She also noted that input for the standards would be broad based, undertaken under generous public scrutiny, and would not be implemented in the manner that they ultimately were. "Our schools will have higher expectations," Bush proclaimed, "Our schools will have greater resources to help meet those goals. Parents will have more information about the schools, and more say in how their children are educated. From this day forward, all students will have a better chance to learn, to excel, and to live out their dreams" (Bush 2002).

Instead, as many of us are painfully aware, NCLB led to a restrictive curriculum, frustrated teachers, a wave of cheating scandals, teaching to the test instead of solid instruction, an overall weakening of public education, and further depriving disadvantaged children of meaningful education (Strauss 2012). The effort to standardize education across the nation has coincided with a profound decline in creativity over the past several decades. It has been productive on one level, however, for it has profoundly increased the wealth of publishing companies, tutoring services, and for-profit education ventures. You see, public education was never broken—it was about the money and control all along.

While the Common Core Standards Initiative appears to be very similar to NCLB, it is actually a completely different monster. Common Core makes NCLB look like a purring little kitten. Obama handed the original national standards plan that was in the works, to a handful of large corporations and the United Nations, who morphed it into the abomination it is today. As we progress through the Core, pay particular attention to the relationships and interests of the various key players, as well as the language used versus the true intent that is lurking in the shadows of the words on the pages.

The Common Core Standards Initiative website has a section for frequently asked questions, and there are a number of them whose answers are…well…not true. I address a number of them throughout this book, starting with the one below.

FAQ: Who was involved in the Common Core State Standards Initiative? States across the country collaborated with teachers, researchers, and leading experts to design and develop the Common Core State Standards. Each state independently made the decision to adopt the Common Core State Standards, beginning in 2010. The federal government was NOT involved in the development of the standards. Local teachers, principals, and superintendents lead the implementation of the Common Core. (Achieve, Common Core State Standards Initiative 2012)

"Local teachers, principals and superintendents" did NOT lead the implementation of Common Core, and states did not collaborate to design them. They did not even know about it until after the Standards had been accepted by the National Governor's Association. The Common Core Standards were developed by an organization called Achieve, both of which are heavily funded by the Gates Foundation (Hardt, Debunking Misconceptions:" The Common Core Was State Led" 2013). Achieve was founded in 1996, according to their website, at the National Education Summit by "leading governors and business leaders," and are funded by various corporations, including the Bill and Melinda Gates Foundation, Microsoft, the Carnegie Corporation of New York, Chevron, Dupont, GE, and IBM. On their "About Us" page on their website, this is what they have to say: "Achieve is proud to be the leading voice for the college- and career-ready agenda, and has helped transform the concept of "college and career readiness for all students" from a radical proposal into a national agenda. Achieve is a bipartisan, non-profit organization that helps states raise academic standards, improve assessments, and strengthen accountability to prepare all young people for postsecondary education, work, and citizenship" (Achieve 2002).

> **Were teachers involved in the creation of the standards? Yes. Teachers have been a critical voice in the development of the standards. The Common Core State Standards drafting process relied on teachers and standards experts from across the country. The National Education Association (NEA), American Federation of Teachers (AFT), National Council of Teachers of Mathematics (NCTM), and National Council of Teachers of English (NCTE), among other organizations were instrumental in bringing together teachers to provide specific, constructive feedback on the standards (Achieve, Common Core State Standards Initiative 2012).**

No, they were not. The authors of the standards themselves are David Coleman, Susan Pimentel and Jason Zimba. The group enticed then Executive Director of CCSSO Gene Wilhoit to climb aboard with assured future employment once his tour of duty with CCSSO was finished. None of the authors are, or have ever been, classroom teachers, nor did they consult with teachers in writing the standards (Author 2013). David Coleman is head of the College Board, and is currently busy rewriting the ACT and SAT so that they align with Common Core as well. He describes the Common Core Standards idea inception by saying "think of a napkin" and "few people in a room with an idea" (Resmovitz 2013). Susan Pimentel started out in Standards setting in 1993 with a Walton Family Foundation grant. She has a law degree, as well as experience consulting in setting standards at the district level, such as Chicago, and states, including Arizona, California, Georgia, Maryland, and Pennsylvania. Susan Pimentel is co-author Raising the Standard: An Eight Step Action Guide For Schools and Communities, funded by The Walton Family Foundation "to lay out the process and content of standards-setting at the community and state levels. The goal was to create a framework in which communities, districts, schools and even states could participate in a self-guided standards-setting process." She is the co-founder of Standardswork and is English Language Arts Consultant at Achieve (Unknown 2013).

None of the authors has an educational background appropriate for designing standards for students from kindergarten through high school, and they know virtually nothing about educational best practices, or teaching these age groups (Swasey 2013). Jason Zimba is a professor of physics and math at Vermont's Bennington College, and says the standards include "an awful lot of algebra before eighth grade," even though the first full course doesn't come until high school. Zimba acknowledges, however, that Common Core algebra does not get much deeper in high school, with no advance mathematics, and could inhibit students from attending many colleges. Common Core is not aligned with the collegiate expectations as claimed. "If you want to take calculus your freshman year in college, you will need to take more mathematics than is in the Common Core," Zimba said (Ravitch, James Milgram on the Common Core Standards 2013).

The Common Core Standards are touted by supporters as being only standards, leaving curriculum choice in the hands of the states and school districts; however, Common Core does include a curriculum that states are strongly "encouraged" to use as well to ensure that students are successful on the tests. "When the tests align with the standards, the curriculum will have to align as well," states Bill Gates (Beck 2013). In other words, states have no choice but to use the federal curriculum to at least have a chance to pass the standardized tests. What's more, the standards are protected by copyright (Achieve 2012) which means they can never be modified—ever. How comfortable are you with corporations writing public policy that cannot be repealed or modified?

According to the government, initiation and development of the Common Core Standards was "state-led" and adoption was "voluntary." The Achieve website, however, tells a different story: "To this day, Achieve remains the only education reform organization led by a Board of Directors of governors and business leaders. This unique perspective has enabled Achieve to set a bold and visionary agenda over the past 15 years, leading Education Week in 2006 to rank Achieve as one of the most influential education policy organizations in the nation. Eventually the creators of the Common Core State Standards Initiative (CCSSI) realized the need to present a facade of state involvement, and therefore, enlisted the National Governors Association (NGA), a trade association that does not include all governors, and the Council of Chief State School Officers (CCSSO), another DC-based trade association. Neither of these groups have grant authority from any particular state or states to write the standards. The bulk of the creative work was done by Achieve, Inc., a DC-based nonprofit that includes many progressive education reformers who have been advocating national standards and curriculum for decades. Massive funding for all this came from private interests such as The Bill and Melinda Gates Foundation" (Achieve 2002).

Does the federal government play a role in standards implementation? The federal government had no role in the development of the Common Core State Standards and will not have a role in their implementation. The Common Core State Standards Initiative is a state-led effort that is not part of No Child Left Behind and adoption of the standards is in no way mandatory (Achieve, Common Core State Standards Initiative 2012).

I cannot emphasize enough that this is not a "state-led" effort, and there was minimal public engagement throughout the process, for the media was eerily silent on the matter until only recently, and Congress, parents, teachers, and local officials were unaware of what was taking place. The Council of Chief State School Officers, and the National Governors Association, approved Common Core in 2010 before the standards were finished being written, and the states were informed about them afterwards (Luksik 2013). This is where the federal government stepped in. In April of this year, the federal government announced that "the Department of Education will oversee the assessment test design for the new national standards" (Given 2013). Whenever assessments control students advancing to the next grade, schools accessing or losing funding, schools closing and teacher's income and job security, the curriculum must follow the test. Since the states were required—not given a choice, but required—to participate in a consortium to develop a common assessment. The choices were the SMARTER Balanced Assessment Consortium and the Partnership for the Assessment of Readiness for College and Careers (PARCC), who subsequently adopted the Common Core Standards and developed the tests themselves (Home School Legal Defense Association 2013), driving another nail in "voluntary's" coffin.

In addition, the states were told upfront that they would lose Title 1 funds if they did not adopt the Common Core Standards 100%, and they also had to adopt the standards if they wanted to apply for Race to the Top funds, completely negating any form of voluntary acceptance. In addition to adopting the national standards and "participating" in a consortia for assessment, states must also implement a longitudinal data collection system that records educational and non-educational information about the student from preschool to age 20, as well as private family data. In 2012 the states were again pushed with a bribe that promised waivers for No Child Left Behind (NCLB), also known as Elementary and Secondary Education Act (ESEA), if they adopted Common Core, again, in its entirety (Home School Legal Defense Association 2013).

Long story short, the states were backed to the edge of the cliff and pressured to jump without knowing what the standards were or what implementing them would entail. Forty-five States originally adopted the Common Core, and signed on with one of two testing consortia, also mandated by the federal government, the Partnership for Assessing Readiness for College and Career (PARCC) or the Smarter Balanced Assessment Consortia (SBAC). States are planning to implement this initiative by 2015 with a minimum of 85% of their state curricula directly from Common Core Standards and "recommended material." Coupled with the millions of dollars in federal funding, many states feel they have no choice but to adopt Common Core, along with its College and Career Ready Standards, workforce skills in the affective domain, moving away from an academic curriculum toward a standards based system designed to produce the ultimate, manufactured global citizen.

Are the standards internationally benchmarked? Yes. International benchmarking played a significant role in both sets of standards. In fact, the college and career ready standards include an appendix listing the evidence that was consulted in drafting the standards and the international data used in the benchmarking process is included in this appendix (Achieve, Common Core State Standards Initiative 2012).

The corporate gurus who wrote the standards claim that they were modelled after the standards from high-performing countries. In reality, the Common Core Standards mimic some of the language, but do not reflect the content. Not one Common Core standard can be matched to any other standard in any other country. The Common Core Standards are unique, untested and unproven, rendering them dangerous.

James Milgram, Professor of Mathematics at Stanford, served on the Common Core validation committee and refused to sign off on the standards. *"I can tell you that my main objection to Core Standards, and the reason I didn't sign off on them was that they did not match up to international expectations. They were at least 2 years behind the practices in the high achieving countries by 7th grade, and, as a number of people have observed, only require partial understanding of what would be the content of a normal, solid, course in Algebra I or Geometry. Moreover, they cover very little of the content of Algebra II, and none of any higher level course… They will not help our children match up to the students in the top foreign countries…"* (Citizen 2013).

He went on to state that the majority of the 29 members of the validation committee were focused on "…things like making the standards as non-challenging as possible. Others were focused on making sure their favorite topics were present and handled in the way they liked." Five of the 29 committee members refused to sign off on them.

Likewise, Professor Sandra Stotsky, who also served on the validation committee, was one of the five committee members who refused to sign off on the Common Core standards because they

were academically inferior, wrote in a letter explaining why:
"...we are regularly told that Common Core's standards are internationally benchmarked. Joel Klein, former head of the New York City schools, most recently repeated this myth in an interview with Paul Gigot, the Wall Street Journal editor, during the first week in June. Not mentioned at all in the interview or the op-ed he co-authored in the WSJ a week later is Klein's current position in a company that does a lot of business with Common Core. An Exxon ad, repeated multiple times during a recently televised national tennis match, also suggested that Common Core's standards were internationally benchmarked. We don't know who influenced Exxon's education director. Gigot never asked Klein what countries we were supposedly benchmarked to. Nor did the Exxon ad name a country to which these standards were supposedly benchmarked. Klein wouldn't have been able to answer, nor could Exxon have named a country because Common Core's standards are not internationally benchmarked. Neither the methodologically flawed study by William Schmidt of Michigan State University, nor the post-Common Core studies by David Conley of the University of Oregon, all funded by the Gates Foundation, have shown that Common Core's content is close to, never mind equal to, the level of the academic content of the mathematics and English standards in high-achieving countries. Moreover, Conley's studies actually contradict the findings of his much earlier pre-Common Core study showing what college faculty in this country expect of entering freshmen in mathematics and English" (Citizen 2013).

> **Who will manage the Common Core State Standards Initiative in the future? The Common Core State Standards Initiative was and will remain a state-led effort. In addition to supporting effective implementation of the Common Core State Standards, NGA and CCSSO are committed to developing a long-term sustainability structure with leadership from governors, chief state school officers, and other state policymakers. There will**

be an ongoing state-led development process that can
support continuous improvement of the standards
(Achieve, Common Core State Standards Initiative 2012).

All the right words, but, as we have already seen, they are a lie. The federal government never intended for education to rest in state and local hands, and devised a scheme to manipulatively tighten federal control over our schools.

The agenda of Common Core became embedded in our education system with NCLB, and it's been pushed on us ever since, and we've pushed back. Older names for Common Core Standards are: Outcome Based Education (OBE), Competency Based Education, Performance Based Education, Mastery Learning Model, and Student Centered Learning. The keys in all of these initiatives lies in each individual learning based on prescribed outcomes or standards (Hoge 2013). This mindset is backwards, and this backward mindset has evolved into a process that has been slowly infiltrating schools over the past several decades. Years of solid research demonstrates that this process is not natural, and, although the word "individual" is used, it does not identify and allow for individual differences in learning and understanding information. The focus is to remove teachers from teaching the curriculum, based on proven methods of instruction, to a group of students, meeting the needs of all intellectual differences. Instead, teachers are to prepare students to meet the needs of the global economy, becoming ideal global citizens—productive, compliant and dependent.

> **FAQ: What makes this process different from other efforts to create common standards? This process is state-led, and has support from across the country, including CCSSO, the NGACenter, Achieve, Inc, ACT, the College Board, the National Association of State Boards of Education, the Alliance for Excellent Education, the Hunt Institute, the National Parent Teacher Association, the State Higher Education**

Executive Officers, the American Association of School Administrators, and the Business Roundtable (Achieve, Common Core State Standards Initiative 2012).

Again, the "state-led" claim. In some ways, it is more of the same. Another program, something new and shiny promising the stars and the moon. In reality, the Common Core Standards transforms education with each student, regardless of varying intellectual capabilities and needs, meeting one controlled set of standards expecting one controlled outcome. Traditional education is turned upside down, and freedoms, as well protections, afforded to us through the Constitution and its amendments, the Bill of Rights, and various laws, are destroyed. As Christopher Tienken, assistant professor of Education Administration at Seton Hall University, expressed it, "…to remain the most creative and nimble economy in the world, the nation must remain as non-standardized as possible. Common standards do not do this. Standards in general attempt to reign in knowledge to what is already known, not expand it or develop the conditions necessary for creating new knowledge…students bring various levels of prior experience, emotions and attitudes to the classroom…we do not see any evidence that standardizing instruction will improve education for children." Common Core mandates that all students meet the same standards. Tienken added that Common Core was created as a response to the claim that public education is hampering our country's global competitiveness. The truth is, "there's no empirical evidence to support it. You can look at test after test, going back to 1964, and find no correlation between test rankings of U.S. students and any indicator of economic prowess, such as per capita GDP or even the Growth Competitiveness Index calculated by the World Economic Forum" (Alexander 2013).

Did you catch the mandate that all students meet the same standards? Let that sink in for a moment. EVERYONE, including special education students, will meet the SAME standard. How many students right now have ADHD, autism, or another cognitive disability that affects how and/or what that student learns?

Clearly, everyone is not the same, and to push an agenda that attempts to force the proverbial square peg into the round hole is, in my, opinion, ludicrous. In addition, the harmful results to these children, as well as to all children, will be insurmountable. This is an unfortunate consequence of socialism, and we are seeing it unfold right now in our schools (Roger 2010). Equitable education sounds like it is making equal opportunity available for all children, which I fully support, but in reality, it is forcing one giant cookie-cutter experience onto every student in this country, and that, I cannot support. Differentiated instruction goes right out the window.

So far, we have plenty of reasons to fight the Common Core Standards, but that's only the beginning. Congress is currently considering a host of bills that have elements of the entire Common Core State Standards Initiative dispersed throughout them. Keep in mind that the authors of controversial proposals do not create bills that are clearly entitled by the issue at hand; rather, those that draft such legislation embed the dubious measures in a bill with a completely different focal point. When I was on govtrack.us last night, I counted over 30 bills that are education-related, but by the titles of some, you would never know it.

Two bills to be especially mindful of: House Bill HR 5 and Senate Bill SB 1094 (Govtrack.us 2013), which shamelessly include "across domain" testing for the social and emotional development of students. Common Core provides for psychoanalysis of students, starting with "screenings" and identification of at risk students, followed by treatment with the school psychologist with referral to outside intervention if it is deemed necessary (Hoge 2013). Should the parent resist, the schools are now mandated to report them to Child Protection Services. This mandate is reflected in Obamacare as well, which specifically outlines the plan for mandatory home visits, particularly targeting a predetermined "at risk" population. The criteria is contained in a manual developed by the Department of Health and Human Services and Child Protective Services, includes families where someone smokes, families where at least one person has ADHD, families with a member who either has served or currently is serving in the military, and families where a child appears to have a development delay, academic difficulties or behavioral difficulties. Where is this information going to come from? From school records. Remember the longitudinal data system that states must develop? The Chief State School Officers recently released the additional dispositions to the standards now called College Career Citizenship Readiness. Attitudes, values, and dispositions included.

HR 5 also provides for charter schools and school choice (Govtrack.us 2013). This will blur tax bases and diminish the existence of public schools. It will also allow the formation of schools for the elite, in spite of the repeated claims of equal education for all. Research the children of the corporate leaders pushing Common Core and see where they go to school., While I read several articles explaining both of these bills and how dangerous they are when combined, an article written by Anne Hodges entitled "Obama's Dream Come True: Nationalizing Education" sums it up best: "funding establishes or expands inter- or intra-district public school choice programs that follow the child starting at birth to age 21, mandates workforce skills, and testing across ALL domains, attitudes and values included. It also establishes a NATIONAL SCHOOL BOARD. This bill, however, does not extend the choice funds to private schools , for the amendment to allow Title I dollars to follow a student to any school, public or private, was defeated (Hoge 2013). The meshing of the two bills provides the entire agenda of burying local control for good and freedom to intrude into the most private of places— your child's heart, mind and soul—coupled with workforce training and assessment from the earliest age possible to the end of life. How free will our children be then?

Forty-five of the fifty states in the United States were originally members of the Common Core State Standards Initiative; however, since the standards were released and the content was accessible, several have now dropped out. States opted in because they were handed an incentive to adopt the Common Core Standards through the competitive federal Race to the Top grants to the tune of $4.35 billion from the Recovery Act. President Obama and Secretary of Education Arne Duncan announced Race to the Top competitive grants on July 24, 2009 (Viteritti 2013), as the carrot. To be eligible, states had to adopt "internationally benchmarked standards and assessments that prepare students for success in college and the work place." This meant that in order for a state to be eligible for these grants, the states had to adopt the Common Core State Standards or something similar (Marybeth Sullivan 2013). The rush to accept federal dollars provided a major push for states to adopt the standards.

> **FAQ: Will there be tests based on the Common Core State Standards? Yes. States that adopted the Common Core State Standards are currently collaborating to develop common assessments that will be aligned to the standards and replace existing end of year state assessments. These assessments will be available in the 2014-2015 school year (Achieve, Common Core State Standards Initiative 2012).**

With the implementation of new standards, states were also required to adopt new assessments. Two consortia surfaced with two different approaches to test the standards. Twenty-six states formed the PARCC RttT Assessment Consortium, (Partnership for Assessment of Readiness for College and Careers, Race to the Top.) The approach focuses on computer-based 'through-course assessments' in each grade combined with streamlined end of year tests, including performance tasks. The second consortium, the SMARTER Balanced Consortium, consists of thirty-one states for adaptive online exams. The decision to use which assessment is determined by state education agencies at this time; however, the end goal is to create one universal assessment system based on the Common Core Standards. This unprecedented move changes the Standardized Testing most students are currently taking, because standardized testing measures content and does not measure attitudes. I am heartened, however, that as of this time, several states, including Utah and Georgia, have withdrawn and are developing their own standardized tests.

Both Democrats and Republicans, as well as Tea Party members, oppose Common Core, with the left primarily opposing the high stakes testing component and the blatant involvement of corporations in the education process, as well as tying teacher contracts to the results of a test that has not even been tested. The right sees these issues, but focuses on constitutional issues such as violating the tenth amendment, the loss of local control of education, the use of non-literary readings which have a propaganda tone, and the focus on "Everyday Math style" non-standard math solutions. The Common Core Standards Initiative brought two opposing forces together to form a large grass roots coalition of opposition.

Although forty-five state originally adopted the Common Core Standards, there has been a growing movement by states to denounce both the standards and consortia. Over this past year, Michigan, Indiana, Georgia, Maine, and Florida have withdrawn from the initiative, or provided local districts with opt out provisions. Several other states, such as Pennsylvania, Florida, and New York, have pending legislation to withdraw, or have governors who have now has the opportunity to review the provisions of the Common Core Standards Initiative and are considering partial or complete withdrawal as well. To this date, eight senators have joined the fight against Common Core as well.

As Carol Burris, principal of South Side High School in New York, wrote in a letter that she co-authored stating her position, as well as that of principals across the state, "When I first read about the Common Core State Standards, I cheered. I believe that our schools should teach all students (except for those who have severe learning disabilities), the skills, habits and knowledge that they need to be successful in post- secondary education. That doesn't mean that every teenager must be prepared to enter Harvard, but it does mean that every young adult, with few exceptions, should at least be prepared to enter their local community college. That is how we give students a real choice…I confess that I was naïve. I should have known in an age in which standardized tests direct teaching and learning, that the standards themselves would quickly become operationalized by tests. Testing, coupled with the evaluation of teachers by scores, is driving its implementation. The promise of the Common Core is dying and teaching and learning are being distorted. The well that should sustain the Core has been poisoned" (Carol Burris 2013). She's not alone. Many, including state governments, bought the bill of goods sold by the NGA, CCSSO, Bill Gates and friends, and the Department of Education.

As yourself this: why is there no transparency or clarity, and why the secretive meetings of the developers of the standards? Why did the federal government feel the need to sneak something in that is supposed to be good for our country and force adoption, and why is there no amendment process for a principal, parent or teacher who sees a problem with these national standards? And why so many lies? If it's that great, why use lies and coercion to sell it?

Philosophical History Shapes Common Core

"In our dream we have limitless resources, and the people yield themselves with perfect docility to our molding hand. The present educational conventions fade from our minds; and, unhampered by tradition, we work our own good will upon a grateful and responsive rural folk. We shall not try to make these people or any of their children into philosophers or men of learning or of science. We are not to raise up among them authors, orators, poets, or men of letters. We shall not search for embryo great artists, painters, musicians. Nor will we cherish even the humbler ambition to raise up from among them lawyers, doctors, preachers, statesmen, of whom we now have ample supply."

- Rev. Frederick T. Gates, Business Advisor to John D. Rockefeller Sr., 1913

It is important to understand not only the historical context, but also the future design, within which Common Core is crafted to understand the initiative's implications, as well as to dissect the language that is used in order to recognize the intent of word selection as well as the true meanings, and to recognize the key players in the Common Core Standards Initiative and why they are involved. The historical roots and the ideology that drives Common Core is not new; rather, it has been advanced with a vengeance for over a century. Although we can go back much further, for the purposes of this book and to keep this brief so that we may move on, I will briefly mention a few key people and organizations who have profoundly impacted American education and helped shape the education policy we are faced with today.

There are several powerhouse families that stand out in our nation's history, and three in particular bear mentioning in relation to education. The Rockefellers, Carnegies and Fords, have been prominent business entities since the beginning of the 1900's, and they have had, and still do have, substantial influence over policy-making as well as education since then (Apollo 2012). Other familiar names ride this bandwagon as well, such as Microsoft, Planned Parenthood, GE, Monsanto and IBM. Each respective foundation has made philanthropic contributions, essential to developing the role of generous benefactor, to education throughout history, not only in the United States, but in other countries such as Africa and South America. They formed various boards, foundations, councils and committees that almost from day one, have transcended economic and educational boundaries. Initial efforts were concentrated in underdeveloped areas of the world, such as Africa, in order to secure not only the resources the US needed for economic domination, but also the human capital, with the required skills, necessary for cooperation as well as a readily-accessible labor force (Malleson 2013). For an .excellent and in-depth history, complete with incredible documentation, I urge you to read "The Deliberate Dumbing Down of America," written by Charlotte Thomson Iserbyt (Iserbyt 2000 Ravenna).

Let me pause here and insert a disclaimer. I recognize that John Dewey, and others, introduced philosophies and ideas that were of benefit to our education system. I completely respect the fact that many people admire his work; however, as it is well documented, some of his beliefs and teachings were, in fact, detrimental, particularly later in life. His theories contributed significantly to the "reform" philosophies we are battling today.

On the education side of the house, progressive educators, largely led by John Dewey, opposed a growing national movement that sought to separate academic education for the few and narrow vocational training for the masses, applying a unifying pattern consistently throughout the educational system. To his credit, Dewey did not advocate for a "commercial minded approach to education in the elementary years." (Novak 1960). During the 1920s, when education turned increasingly to "scientific" techniques such as intelligence testing and cost-benefit management, progressive educators insisted on the importance of the emotional, artistic, social, and creative aspects of human development. After the Depression began, the country began to see a blending of these two philosophies when a group of politically-oriented progressive educators, led by George Counts, dared schools to "build a new social order" and published a journal called The Social Frontier to promote their view of social reconstruction, or "The pedagogical philosophy …simply rests on the idea that schools need to shape or "reconstruct" society (Westheimer 2011). Edward Thorndike, who created the field of educational philosophy, established that education in specific disciplines such as history, philosophy and rhetoric, created an independent and intellectual individual who is difficult to manipulate. At Teachers College, Columbia University, William H. Kilpatrick and other students of Dewey taught the principles of progressive education to thousands of teachers and school leaders, and in the middle part of the century, books such as Dewey's Experience and Education (1938) Boyd Bode's Progressive Education at the Crossroads (1938), Caroline Pratt's I Learn from Children (1948), and Carlton Washburne's What is Progressive Education? (1952) among others, continued to mold teachers, shaping their values and beliefs about their roles in education and what the ideal outcome should, by progressive standards, be (Thomlinson 2005). As with any seed that is planted and nurtured, these ideas grew, until the seemingly benign focus on individuality and the creative spirit grew into a utopian and controlling vision of an ideal and productive world citizenship.

John Dewey, often called the "father of progressive education," co-authored the first Humanist Manifesto with a socialist agenda, advocating for a "synthesizing of all religions…Any religion that can hope to be a synthesizing and dynamic force for today, must be shaped for the needs of this age." Socialism is a political and economic theory of social re-organization that believes that the means of production, distribution, and exchange should be owned or regulated by the community (government) as a whole. In other words, everybody has the same amount of wealth, the same values, the same goals, and a centralized government defines the parameters for each. It stifles individual motivation and achievement, as well as competition. The goal is to prevent one student from being perceived as superior to another (Dewey's Political Philosophy 2005). The Humanist Manifesto uses the same carefully selected language to sell its belief system that we see with federal government today, with Common Core and Obamacare being two prime examples.

Dewey was a cohort of John D. Rockefeller, and joined the faculty of the University of Chicago, which was heavily funded by Rockefeller. Over the years, Dewey came to the conclusion that schools should "build the curriculum not around academic subjects but around occupational activities which provided maximum opportunities for peer interaction and socialization." Dewey believed that the commitment to literacy in our nation's schools was a problem that needed to be "solved", otherwise it would continue to inhibit industrial and social "progress." Dewey envisioned a workforce of citizens who had been properly groomed with the correct attitudes, both socially and politically, and would not question authority. Again, the schools were to be geared toward preparing students for work, and to think of themselves as a functional part of a larger machine, not promoting literacy or individual talents, goals, or achievements. Dewey believed that school for the sake of learning was simply a waste of time. His socialization beliefs helped perpetuate the goal of everybody being the same. Learning should "be active, not passive," a child should be "in possession of his fullest talents" and "school should be social rather than individualist." Further, he believed that schools were to "enable a child to think creatively, experimentation rather than imitation should be encouraged," and are all defined within the context of what he, and others, decided this should look like. The government, reminiscent of Nazi

Germany, China and Russia, would decide what creativity and what the child's fullest talents would be, and how they would be used, not the child or family (James Millgram 2013). Achievement was discouraged, for one student doing better than others would make the others "feel bad" leading to a less-than-ideal social situation. Level everything out and everyone feels good and gets along, right? Parents were, and apparently still are, considered incapable of raising their children on their own, and needed "professionals" to help them.

The Progressive Education Association met on December 28, 1928 to develop a plan to dumb-down American students by instituting a new math program, which was developed in less than two hours. The meeting was chaired by a Dr. Ziegler of the Education Committee of the Council on Foreign Relations, a group formed for the purpose of destroying the national sovereignty of the United States and to unite all existing countries under a New World Order. Drs. John Dewey and Edward Thorndike, documented paid members of the Communist Party of Russia, were part of that meeting. Dr. Ziegler is documented in meeting notes as saying to O.A. Nelson, then vice principal of Wilson High School in Minneapolis, Minnesota, who initially questioned the new math program, "Nelson, wake up! That is what we want, a math that the pupils cannot apply to life situations when they get out of school!" Wilson is later quoted as saying "That math was not introduced until much later, as those present [at the meeting in 1928] thought it was too radical a change. A milder course by Dr. Breckner was substituted, but it was also worthless, as far as understanding math was concerned. The radical change was introduced in 1952. It was the one [form of new math] we are using now. So, if pupils come out of high school now, not knowing any math, don't blame them. The results are supposed to be worthless (101 2008)." There has been a movement to dumb down American citizens for a long time, and is only now becoming obvious.

Inherent in not only education but also the Common Core assessments is Howard Gardner's theory of Multiple Intelligences. Gardner was a professor and neuroscientist at Harvard, and he postulated that humans are not limited to one uniform cognitive capacity; rather, there are nine different intelligences scattered among human beings, displayed differently from individual to individual. Consequently, humans interact with the world differently and cannot be expected to provide the same objective answers to a set of questions. He argued that assessment should reflect the differences in these intelligences, and this relativism is overtly seen in the new assessments focus on open-ended questions. Howard Gardner's Multiple Intelligences Theory. Gardner also advocated for comprehensive tracking of student performance, also reflected in the Common Core's intense data tracking structure.

There have been others whose philosophies have wound their way into our education system via corporations and public policy. Benjamin Bloom's "Taxonomy of Educational Standards" was written to serve "…as a tool to classify the ways individuals are to act, think or feel as the result of participating in some unit of instruction." Bloom maintained that educators were responsible for influencing how "individuals should act, think or feel" and to assist education's purpose to "integrate beliefs, ideas, and attitudes into a total philosophy or world view." The Partners for 21st Century Skills is actually proud to be based on Bloom's theories. I find the fact that our corporate elites who are trying to shove Common Core down our throats hold Bloom out to be a hero. Common Core is, indeed, focused on teaching the "right" attitudes and values, their attitudes and values, and even aims to gather tremendous amounts of private data about students and their families to do so (HSDLA 2013). Much of what children learned at home was undesirable, creating the perception that schools needed to "reprogram them" and what better way to do so than through a compulsory program that occupied the majority of a child's waking hours for the better part of a week?

Who Stands to Gain from Common Core?

"Students who acquire large debts putting themselves through school are unlikely to think about changing society, Chomsky suggested. *"When you trap people in a system of debt, they can't afford the time to think." Tuition fee increases are a "disciplinary technique," and, by the time students graduate, they are not only loaded with debt, but have also internalized the "disciplinarian culture." This makes them efficient components of the consumer economy."* –Noam Chomsky

FAQ: Will CCSSO and NGA be creating common instructional materials and curricula? States that have adopted the standards may choose to work together to develop instructional materials and curricula. As states join together to adopt the same Common Core State Standards, publishers of instructional materials and experienced educators will develop new resources around these shared standards (Achieve, Common Core State Standards Initiative 2012).

Why are large corporations and organizations investing huge amounts of money in Common Core? Nobody invests money unless they expect a return on that investment. Many proponents happen to be corporations and non-profits that are increasing revenues by implementing texts, tools, curricula and professional development for the Common Core. In addition, they are promoting a "sustainable global economy," meaning profiting by pushing common education to create their idea of a utopian world market. Remember the Bill Gates quote "…identifying common standards is just the starting point. We will only know if this effort has succeeded when the curriculum and tests are aligned to these standards … When the tests are aligned to the common standards, the curriculum will line up as well, and it will unleash a

powerful market of people providing services for better teaching."
As the Wall Street Journal reported in May of 2012 a statement by
the Thomas B. Fordham Institute that "the price tag could be as
high as $1 billion to $8 billion" with most of that money going to
publishing companies (Fleisher 2012).

"Education reform" is another phrase that we really
have to scrutinize to discern the truth. "Corporate reform" is more
accurate, for the goal is clearly not what is best for the students;
rather, it is what is best for entrepreneurship and the global
marketplace. Hence, the primary funders of "education reform" are
corporations and nonprofits who collaborate with the US
Department of Education, and who all stand something to gain.
The funders advocate for measures that seek to eliminate the local
control purposefully mandated by the Constitution, turning the
education system into a factory for profits and workers. This is a
major reason why there are constant references to providing
students with skills necessary to be effective citizens, leaders and
workers, as well as the repeated use of "career ready," "global
economy," "competitive workforce," and "21st century skills."
Words that sell, and profit-mongers are buying our children to add
to their bottom line.

Pearson, for instance, already the largest online book
company in the world, has already been producing new textbooks
and new curriculum, and is the sole producer of the ebooks that are
to replace regular books. Not only that, but take a look at a
statement made in their 2012 earnings report: "The Partnership for
Assessment of Readiness for College and Careers
(PARCC)...awarded Pearson and Educational Testing Service
(ETS) the contract to develop test items that will be part of the new
English and Mathematics assessments to be administered from the
2014-2015 school year. We continued to produce strong growth in
secure online testing, an important market for the future. We
increased online testing volumes by more than 10%, delivering 6.5
million state accountability tests, 4.5 million constructed response
items and 21 million spoken tests. We now assess oral proficiency

in English, Spanish, French, Dutch, Arabic and Chinese. We also launched the Online Assessment Readiness Tool for the PARCC and the Smarter Balance Assessment Consortium (SBAC) Common Core consortia to help 45 states prepare for the transition to online assessments" (Pearson, Inc. 2013). Pearson's website proudly notes "Pearson's close association with key authors and architects of the Common Core State Standards ensures that the spirit and pedagogical approach of the initiative is embodied in our professional development" (Pearson, Inc. 2013). It is interesting to note that, Kathy Hurley, Senior Vice President of Strategic Partnerships for Pearson Education and partners with CCSSO in implementing the Common Core State Standards, is also Executive Chair for the Partnership for 21st Century Skills. Is anybody seeing some serious conflict of interest yet?

Let me take a moment to introduce you to ALEC. ALEC, or the American Legislative Exchange Council, with membership consisting of almost 2000 state legislators and funded by large corporations, was founded in 1973 by Paul Weyrich (Center for Media and Democracy 2012). Weyrich defined ALEC's primary objectives as an effort to downsize government and loosen regulation on corporations, shifting power to "the elite," and to make it as difficult as possible to hold the economically and politically powerful accountable. He wrote a manual called The Despoiling of America to teach his followers how to gain and retain power over the country. Here are four principles from his book: (1) Falsehoods are not only acceptable, they are a necessity. The corollary is: The masses will accept any lie if it is spoken with vigor, energy and dedication. (2) It is necessary to be cast under the cloak of "goodness" whereas all opponents and their ideas must be cast as "evil." (3) Complete destruction of every opponent must be accomplished through unrelenting personal attacks. 4) The creation of the appearance of overwhelming power and brutality is necessary in order to destroy the will of opponents to launch opposition of any kind (Yurica 2004). http://www.yuricareport.com/Dominionism/TheDespoilingOfAmer

ica.htm. Eric Heubeck, who authored Weyrich's manual, introduces the book with this:

> "There will be three main stages in the unfolding of this movement. The first stage will be devoted to the development of a highly motivated elite able to coordinate future activities. The second stage will be devoted to the development of institutions designed to make an impact on the wider elite and a relatively small minority of the masses. The third stage will involve changing the overall character of American popular culture…Our movement will be entirely destructive, and entirely constructive. We will not try to reform the existing institutions. We only intend to weaken them, and eventually destroy them. We will endeavor to knock our opponents [sic] off-balance and unsettle them at every opportunity. All of our constructive energies will be dedicated to the creation of our own institutions…We will maintain a constant barrage of criticism against the Left. We will attack the very legitimacy of the Left. We will not give them a moment's rest. We will endeavor to prove that the Left does not deserve to hold sway over the heart and mind of a single American. We will offer constant reminders that there is an alternative, there is a better way. When people have had enough of the sickness and decay of today's American culture, they will be embraced by and welcomed into the New Traditionalist movement. The rejection of the existing society by the people will thus be accomplished by pushing them and pulling them simultaneously…We will use guerrilla tactics to undermine the legitimacy of the dominant regime…We must create a countervailing force that is just as adept as the Left at intimidating people and institutions that are used as tools of left-wing activism but are not ideologically committed, such as Hollywood celebrities, multinational corporations, and university administrators. We must be feared, so that they will think

twice before opening their mouths…We will be results-oriented rather than good intentions-oriented. Making a good-faith effort and being ideologically sound will be less important than advancing the goals of the movement…We need more people with fire in the belly, and we need a message that attracts those kinds of people…We must reframe this struggle as a moral struggle, as a transcendent struggle, as a struggle between good and evil. And we must be prepared to explain why this is so. We must provide the evidence needed to prove this using images and simple terms… (K. Yurica 2004)"

That has a familiar feeling to it, doesn't it?

The basic modus operandi of this secretive organization is to use corporate funders' money to write self-serving legislation and ensure it is made into law in states across the country. ALEC buys states (Nichols 2011), and they operated largely off anyone's radar until the Trayvon Martin case. As it turns out, ALEC created the "Stand Your Ground" legislation that allowed George Zimmerman to kill Trayvon, an unarmed teenager, claiming that he "felt threatened." This case caused light to be shone on the entire organization and its underhanded dealings over the past several decades. As a result, a number of corporations, including Kraft, Coca-Cola, the Bill and Melinda Gates Foundation, and Intuit, have dropped out; however, ALEC still has a number of powerhouse members, including the Koch brothers, Walmart, and AT&T. The reason I am telling you all of this? ALEC, particularly when Bill Gates was providing substantial funds, was the driving force behind common education in the US. Although Gates and others recently severed ties with ALEC, the organization is still a formidable antagonist in the Common Core agenda.

Bill Gates is the biggest advocate for Common Core, not just in terms of support, but in terms of dollars, as well. Gates funds a number of special interest groups, such as the League of

Education Voters, Student Achievement Partners, the American Federation of Teachers, the Association for Supervision and Curriculum Development, the Harvard Education Letter, the National Congress of Parents and Teachers, the Education Trust, the National Association of Education, the Center for Reinventing Public Education and The Partnership for Learning, all Common Core advocates; Gates owns Editorial Projects in Education, parent of Education Week magazine (Schneider 2013). Many educators do not have a full understanding of what Common Core really is, and it does not surprise me. Educators access resources created by Bill Gates and corporate partners who want their buy-in, with Education Week and the Harvard Education Letter as two prime examples. Not only that, Gates is currently searching for a $250,000 grant recipient to sell Common Core to the education community (Swasey, Top Ten Scariest People in Education Reform #5-Bill Gates 2013). Wherever there is support for Common Core, Gates' influence is at the helm. For instance, he handed a million dollars to the national PTA to advocate for Common Core with parents, and he gave Common Core developer NGA/CCSSO approximately $25 million for promotion purposes. Gates also provided Harvard with $15 million for "education policy" research, and $9 million more went to universities to promote "breakthrough learning models" and global education. In addition, Gates paid InBloom $100 million to gather data from pilot schools as part of a collaboration designed to develop "shared technology services" (Empson 2013) InBloom, which used to be known as the Shared Learning Collaborative, includes the unelected Council of Chief State School Officers (CCSSO) as well as states and districts.

It is difficult to lay everything out neatly to create a clear picture of how much money is being spent on Common Core and by whom, and I am certain that is intentional. I am going to pick on Bill Gates some more because he has his hands—and his money— in every aspect of education everywhere, it just isn't always apparent. For instance, Gates gave $3 million to Stanford

University and $3 million to Brown University for "college and career readiness," (Schneider, Gates Money and Common Core-Part IV 2013)which clearly is part of the Common Core agenda, especially considering the fact that "college and career readiness" is the government's classic way of referring to Common Core. Sometimes he's promoting "support activities around educational issues related to school reform" for the CCSSO and other times he's "helping states build data interoperability," otherwise known as data mining. Gates has admitted to spending five billion dollars to promote his educational experiment since 2000.

David Coleman is another one to watch carefully. Unlike Gates, Coleman operates more in the shadows. It bears noting, however, a little transaction he was involved in earlier this year. David Coleman has been the CEO of Grow Industries, a company that provides customized test reports and instructional materials for educators, as well as students and families. The company was recently purchased by McGraw-Hill Education (Horn 2012). The purpose is to create a company who can provide a full range of customized education solutions to help improve teaching and learning. "Grow will work closely with other divisions within McGraw-Hill Education, including CTB/McGraw-Hill, the nation's leading provider of assessments, to offer services that are tailored to meet school districts' specific curriculum, assessment, and reporting needs. Grow also will continue to work with other assessment programs selected by its state and school district partners." David Coleman, its chief executive officer, and his team will remain in place. "We chose McGraw-Hill Education as our home because of the exceptional quality of its assessments and the distinctive depth of its instructional materials. Together with the McGraw-Hill team, Grow can make even more powerful linkages between assessment and instruction that significantly improve teaching and learning," Coleman said (Ravitch, David Coleman: The Most Influential Man in Education? 2013).

Teach for America, largely supported by ALEC, is technically a nonprofit organization that recruits college graduates, regardless of major, provides five weeks of training over the summer, and then sends them to teach in poor schools. They receive periodic financial boosts a la Common Core as well (Mayer 2012). I say technically, for they bring in enough money to make a profit and then some, easily meeting all of their objectives, including high salaries for those at the helm. Walmart's Walton family handed them $20 million this past August to continue creating its "pipeline of outstanding education reform leaders" (Layton 2013). I thought they were supposed to be teaching? That's not all. Teach for America produces unqualified "teachers" that are replacing veteran teachers because it is cheaper, they are prepared to teach what corporate reformers want them to teach, and they are not unionized (Rubenstein 2013). Teach for America is a manufacturing plant designed to crank out a large quantity of teachers cheaply. These are the teachers the average child will ultimately receive their "public" education from, while the best teachers, the ones who are truly qualified, will be wooed to the elite schools, and compensated well, making it an offer that can't be refused, for these teachers will likely have families they have to support, so saying "no" will not be an option.

Valerie Strauss, a Harvard graduate heavily pursued by Teach for America, turned them down after doing her research. "Indeed, in my experience Harvard students have increasingly acknowledged that TFA drastically underprepares its recruits for the reality of teaching. But more importantly, TFA is not only sending young, idealistic, and inexperienced college grads into schools in neighborhoods different from where they're from—it's also working to destroy the American public education system. As a hopeful future teacher, that is not something I could ever conscionably put my name behind…Districts pay thousands in fees to TFA for each corps member in addition to their salaries—at the expense of the existing teacher workforce. Chicago, for example, is closing 48 schools and laying off 850 teachers and staff while welcoming 350 corps members" (Strauss, Harvard Student: Don't Teach for America 2013).   Teach for America moves in after public schools are closed and often re-opened as charter schools, as was the case in Chicago. Louisiana implemented a similar plan after Hurricane Katrina when the state laid off over 7,000 employees and turned 102 of 117 city schools in charter schools that were nonunionized. Teach for America again provided the lion's share of replacement teachers (McCauley 2013).

There are other corporations on the Common Core money train as well, including Legos, Crayola, Microsoft, Google, Planned Parenthood, the PTA, Exxon, IBM, GE, Charles Schwab, British Petroleum, Citibank, General Mills, Lowes, Monsanto, Hewlett-Packard, SurveyMonkey, Yale University, JP Morgan Chase, US Bank, Williams-Sonoma, Visa, Federal Express, Hostess, and Wells Fargo. Every one of them funds Pearson and/or Teach for America, or both. "These people all know each other," said Michael T. Moore, a literacy professor at Georgia Southern University who has written extensively about Common Core. "It is a private club" (Downey 2013).

Bottom line, our schools are being transformed into new markets for corporations, career training centers, and centers of indoctrination to create "global citizens" with all the right behaviors, attitudes and beliefs, otherwise known as puppets.

Unholy Alliances

"If you tell a lie big enough and keep repeating it, people will eventually come to believe it. The lie can be maintained only for such time as the State can shield the people from the political, economic and/or military consequences of the lie. It thus become vitally important for the State to use all of its powers to repress dissent, for the truth is the mortal enemy of the lie, and thus by extension, the truth is the greatest enemy of the State." –Joseph Goebbels, Hitler's Minister of Propaganda

Have you ever wondered why, since the Common Core pundits clamor on about being "state led," the United Nations is smack dab in the middle of everything? I don't recall the UN having anything to do with anything that goes on in my state…just sayin'.

And that brings me back to Bill Gates. Our friend Bill is partners with the UN Educational, Scientific and Cultural Organization (UNESCO) and is on the UN's Committee for Global Education Standards, which gave birth to the idea of common global education standards (Kibler 2013). Bill Gates has also purchased his way into the UN, completely bypassing the General Assembly approval, by funding a newly-created position and appointing a Bill and Melinda Gates Foundation board and advisory panel member "Ban Ki-moon on June 7, 2012 announced with fanfare -- on the UN's own UN News Service -- that he 'appointed Ms. Amina J. Mohammed of Nigeria as his Special Adviser on Post-2015 Development Planning,' it was not disclosed that this position is not in the UN Budget and will be funded from outside (Lee 2012). The other pillar of the Gates Empire, Microsoft, obtained a position with the UN as its Ambassador to Africa, who also happens to be related to Ban Ki-moon's then Special Adviser on Africa. Hmmmmmm…

UNESCO is a specialized agency of the U.N. system that promotes collaboration among its member countries in the fields of education, natural sciences, social and human sciences, culture, and communications and information. The US played a significant role in forming UNESCO, but its support has wavered during its tenure. With an annual budget of approximately $326 million, UNESCO supports more than 2,000 staff members working at its headquarters in Paris and 65 field offices and institutes worldwide (The United Nations Educational, Scientific and Culteral Organization (UNESCO) 2013). UNESCO activities are funded through a combination of assessed contributions by member states to its regular budget, and voluntary contributions by member states and organizations.

The United States is currently a member of UNESCO and generally supports the organization's objectives. That was not always the case. Over the years, some U.S. policymakers—particularly Members of Congress—expressed strong concern about UNESCO's philosophies, politics and anti-democratic leanings, as well as a lack of sound fiscal management. These concerns led to the United States' decision to withdraw support from UNESCO between 1984 and 2003. In spite of this, members of Congress and corporations, largely Bill Gates, have continued to support UNESCO—providing between $73 million and $84 million in assessed contributions per fiscal year, or about 22% of UNESCO's annual regular budget. The US was number three of the top ten funders of global education in 2011 (Financing for Global Education 2013), and in 2013, the US provided $439 million in the form of 12 grants to support the national education plans of 12 foreign countries, (Global Partnership for Education, Media Center 2013). Support included members maintaining an ongoing interest in ensuring UNESCO runs as efficiently and effectively as possible, and that its policies and programs are in line with US priorities, or that US priorities are in line with UNESCO's policies and programs.

The Obama Administration talks out of both sides of its mouth with regard to UNESCO. On the one hand, it actively opposes Palestinian membership in UNESCO, arguing that Palestinian statehood can only be realized through direct negotiation between Israel and Palestinians, and not through membership in international organizations (No Money, No Vote: A Closer Look at the Strained Relationship Between the U.S. and UNESCO 2013). On the other hand, the Administration maintained that the US would continue participation in UNESCO, as it is considered to be in the best interest of the United States, and that the government would continue to fund and participate in the organization. In his FY2013 budget proposal, President Obama requested $77 million in assessed contributions for UNESCO and stated that the Administration intended to work with Congress to "waive" the funding restrictions. UNESCO critics, however, argue that waiving the laws would undermine U.S. credibility and encourage the Palestinians to continue to pursue membership in other U.N. entities (Shaw 2013). This has not stopped Obama. As a matter of fact, during his campaign in 2008, Obama committed to the US paying for education for all of the world, thoroughly discussed in "A Global Fund for Education: Achieving Education for All." More recently, Hillary Clinton called for a new design of global cooperation that requires institutions to "combine the efficiency and capacity for action with inclusiveness" (A Global Fund for Education: Achieving Education for All 2009). Obama is asking for $501 million for basic education on under the guise of "foreign aid" for FY2014 (House Subcommittee Maintains Funding for Basic Education 2013). To that end, President Barack Obama, Bill Gates, large corporations and organizations, as well as the U.S. Department of Education have used the UN human rights common core to push the Common Core State Standards Initiative into our schools, onto our children and homes, aiming to completely transform America.

The framework for the Common Core Standards was set by the United Nations in their plan for creating their idea of an ideal global society, all of which is chronicled in Agenda 21. I encourage you to download it and read it (United Nations 1992). Chapter 36 of Agenda 21, entitled "Promoting Education, Public Awareness and Training," states its basis for action as this:

Education, including formal education, public awareness and training should be recognized as a process by which human beings and societies can reach their fullest potential. Education is critical for promoting sustainable development and improving the capacity of the people to address environment and development issues. While basic education provides the underpinning for any environmental and development education, the latter needs to be incorporated as an essential part of learning. Both formal and non-formal education are indispensable to changing people's attitudes so that they have the capacity to assess and address their sustainable development concerns. It is also critical for achieving environmental and ethical awareness, values and attitudes, skills and behaviour consistent with sustainable development and for effective public participation in decision-making. To be effective, environment and development education should deal with the dynamics of both the physical/biological and socio-economic environment and human (which may include spiritual) development, should be integrated in all disciplines, and should employ formal and non-formal methods and effective means of communication (United Nations 1992).

The first sentence sounds fabulous, echoing the language of progressive education; however, "Education is critical for promoting sustainable development and improving the capacity of the people to address environment and development issues" clearly has nothing to do with academics, instead, delineates a political emphasis on economics. While that ideology raises red flags, the plan for "changing people's attitudes...critical for achieving environment and development education should deal with the dynamics of both the physical/biological and socio-economic environment and human (which may include spiritual) development, should be integrated in all disciplines, and should employ formal and non-formal methods and effective means of communication" sets emergency warning systems on full red alert. Are you, as a parent, comfortable with not just our government, but large corporations and other governments under the United Nations umbrella, writing our educational system's goals and standards to meet their world development mission? Well, that's what has happened.

Remember that Bill Gates has funded every aspect of Common Core, over $100 million so far, including the development, the evaluation, the implementation, and the advocacy (COMMON CORE MOVEMENT IS A TROJAN HORSE AND TIED TO THE UNITED NATIONS 2013). In 2004, Microsoft, signed a cooperative agreement with the UNESCO. In the cooperative agreement, Gates stated, "Microsoft supports the objectives of UNESCO as stipulated in UNESCO's constitution and intends to contribute to UNESCO's program priorities" (UNESCO, Microsoft, Bill Gates 2004). UNESCO's program to create a global education community, Education for All, is driven by their key document called "The Dakar Framework for Action: Education for All: Meeting Our Collective Commitments." I encourage you to download it and read through it as well (UNESCO 2000).

The agreement stipulated, among other things, that Microsoft will develop a "master curriculum for teacher training in information technologies based on standards, guidelines, benchmarks, and assessment techniques." The Agreement also states that the curriculum will "form the basis for deriving training content to be delivered to teachers," and "UNESCO will explore how to facilitate content development." The curriculum replaces local control, dictates what is taught to students, and dismisses the provisions of the U.S. Constitution and the founders' intent, disguised in feel-good language siting inclusivity, education and tolerance for all the children of the world. In addition, Microsoft clarifies that it collaborates in four of UNESCO's core pillars— education, science, culture, and communication and information— as well as the Education for All agenda. The partners place a primary focus on the global Education for All (EFA) movement, which aims to meet the personalized learning needs of all children, youth, and adults by 2015.

Education for All outlines the theory and activities of global education, states "Prior to the reform of the global EFA coordination architecture in 2011-2012, the Education for All High-Level Group brought together high-level representatives from national governments, development agencies, UN agencies, civil society and the private sector. Its role was to generate political momentum and mobilize financial, technical and political support towards the achievement of the EFA goals and the education-related Millennium Development Goals (MDGs). From 2001-2011 the High-Level Group met annually" (BILL GATES SPENDING MILLIONS ON COMMON CORE DEVELOPMENT AND PROMOTION 2013).

The goals of Education for All were sold with the promise that they were agreed upon internationally. The goals are certainly admirable at first glance; however, they are lofty, and with the attempted implementation of such lofty goals, particularly on a global basis, comes the risk of conflict and control issues. The six goals of Education for All are:

Goal 1 Expanding and improving comprehensive early childhood care and education, especially for the most vulnerable and disadvantaged children.

Goal 2 Ensuring that by 2015 all children, particularly girls, children in difficult circumstances and those belonging to ethnic minorities, have access to, and complete, free and compulsory primary education of good quality.

Goal 3 Ensuring that the learning needs of all young people and adults are met through equitable access to appropriate learning and life-skills programmes.

Goal 4 Achieving a 50 per cent improvement in levels of adult literacy by 2015, especially for women, and equitable access to basic and continuing education for all adults.

Goal 5 Eliminating gender disparities in primary and secondary education by 2005, and achieving gender equality in education by 2015, with a focus on ensuring girls' full and equal access to and achievement in basic education of good quality.

Goal 6 Improving all aspects of the quality of education and ensuring excellence of all so that recognized and measurable learning outcomes are achieved by all, especially in literacy, numeracy and essential life skills (Education for All-History Unknown).

With billions of dollars being poured into these efforts, the corporations, organizations and governments facilitating the realization of these goals are not doing so out of the goodness of their hearts. It is an investment, and the investor always wants something in return.

Education For All, like the other programs mentioned, is based on Agenda 21. On the Education and Awareness page of the U.N. website, you will learn: "Education, Public Awareness and

Training is the focus of Chapter 36 of Agenda 21. This is a cross-sectoral theme both relevant to the implementation of the whole of Agenda 21 and indispensable."

They admit that education is indispensable for the U.N. to foist its agenda onto every citizen worldwide. They want control of what is taught worldwide. Control education, you control minds—and thoughts, values and belief systems.

Referring back to Agenda 21, Chapter 36, in section 36.2, it is written that we should "reorient" worldwide education toward sustainable development. It does not say that we should discuss or vote on, and it provides for no input on this philosophy. Common Core has followed this blue print. Section 36.3 goes on to say: "Both formal and non-formal education are indispensable to changing people's attitudes…. It is also critical for achieving environmental and ethical awareness, values and attitudes, skills and behaviour consistent with sustainable development… To be effective, environment and development education should deal with the dynamics of both the physical/biological and socio-economic environment and human (which may include spiritual) development, should be integrated in all disciplines, and should employ formal and non-formal methods"

The stated objectives in section 36.4 include endorsing Education for All, and "giving special emphasis to the further training of decision makers at all levels." Hence the need for people like Gates to influence the training of decision makers. When asked recently in an interview what matters most to him, Gates said it was education. His version of education, that is. The Huffington Post carried the interview in which he stated, "I'd pick education, if I was thinking broadly about America," Gates responded. "It's our tool of equality" (Huffington Post 2013). Is it coincidence that equality and redistribution are also concepts Arne Duncan is promoting with Common Core?

Just how committed is Bill Gates to the United Nations staying parked in the middle of American education? In his annual letter for 2013, Gates emphasized the importance of following the United Nations' Millennial Goals and measuring teachers more closely (Gates 2013). Remember, one of those UN Millennial Goals is to achieve universal education. Gates recounts the Millennial Goals in the 2013 Annual Letter. Also, Gates helped create Strong American Schools (a successor to the STAND UP campaign launched in 2006, which was an outgrowth of UNESCO's Millennium Campaign Goals for Universal Education (Julian 2013). It called for U.S. national education standards. The seeds for Common Core were planted long ago.

I want to note here also, that Gates' Foundation funded the International Benchmarking Advisory Group (County 2013) , as well as the development of report for Common Core Standards on behalf of the National Governors Association, Council of Chief State School Officers, and ACHIEVE, Inc. titled, "Benchmarking for Success: Ensuring U.S. Students Receive a World-Class Education" (Achieve, Inc. 2008). This report showed the United Nations is a member of the International Benchmarking Advisory Group for Common Core Standards. Why is the UN on an advisory group for the US education system? Remember, too, that the claim that the standards are internationally benchmarked has since been proven false.

Gates is not alone in his UN/UNESCO allegiance. Like all of the other big money interests pushing and profiting from Common Core, Pearson openly supports the UN's Millennium Goals as well. Sir Michael Barber of Pearson noted, "Eradicating extreme poverty continues to be one of the main challenges of our time, and is a major concern of the international community. Ending this scourge will require the combined efforts of all, governments, civil society organizations and the private sector, in the context of a stronger and more effective global partnership for development. The Millennium Development Goals set time bound targets, by which progress in reducing income poverty, hunger, disease, lack of adequate shelter and exclusion — while promoting gender equality, health, education and environmental sustainability

— can be measured. They also embody basic human rights — the rights of each person on the planet to health, education, shelter and security. The Goals are ambitious but feasible and, together with the comprehensive United Nations development agenda, set the course for the world's efforts to alleviate extreme poverty by 2015" (Swasey, Top Ten Scariest People in Education Reform #7-Sir Michael Barber 2013).

There is a plethora of official documentation and reports that delineate the global market creation goals and education being the movement's most important tool. As you read through some of them, the common threads of ideology will be crystal clear.

For instance, the federal government's Equity and Excellence Commission Report reads "But American schools must do more than ensure our future economic prosperity; they must foster the nation's civic culture and sense of common purpose, and create the unified nation that e pluribus unum celebrates. So much depends on fulfilling this mission: the shared ideals that enable our governmental system to hold together even in the face of fractious political disagreements; the strength of our diversity; the domestic tranquility that our Constitution promises; and the ability to maintain the influence—as example and power—that America has long projected in the world. We neglect those expectations at our peril…. Imagine what we could achieve if we made American public schools competitive with those of a higher-performing country such as Canada in mathematics (which means scoring approximately 40 points higher on PISA tests) over the next 20 years. As our higher-skill-level students entered the labor force, they would produce a faster-growing economy. How much faster? The potential is stunning. The improvement in our GDP over the next 80 years would exceed a present value of $70 trillion. That's equivalent to an average 20 percent boost in income for every U.S. worker each year over his or her entire career. This would generate enough revenue to solve the U.S. debt problem that is the object of so much current debate (Swasey, What's Wrong With Social Justice: Rabbi Lapin Explains 2013).

The federal agenda has not been hidden. Arne Duncan gave a speech to UNESCO at a 2010 meeting in France entitled "**The Vision of Education Reform in the United States**." Here are the highlights: "My department has been pleased to partner with the US Agency for International Development to help ensure that our best domestic practices are shared world-wide. The United States provides over a billion dollars annually to partner countries working on educational reform. Our goal for the coming year will be to work closely with global partners, including UNESCO, to promote qualitative improvements and system strengthening....Ultimately, education is the great equalizer. It is the one force that can consistently overcome differences in background, culture, and privilege... Education is still the key to eliminating gender inequities, to reducing poverty, to creating a sustainable planet, and to fostering peace. And in a knowledge economy, education is the new currency by which nations maintain economic competitiveness and global prosperity... Educating girls and integrating them into the labor force is especially critical to breaking the cycle of poverty. It is hard to imagine a better world without a global commitment to providing better education for women and youth—including the 72 million children who do not attend primary school today...The North Star guiding the alignment of our cradle-to-career education agenda is President Obama's goal that America will once again have the highest proportion of college graduates in the world. That goal can only be achieved by creating a strong cradle-to-career continuum that starts with early childhood learning and extends all the way to college and careers... The first assurance was that states would work toward developing academic standards that truly show if a student is ready for college and a career when they graduate from high school. Under the existing system, many states had dummied down academic standards to make students look proficient. While that helps politicians look good, it was bad for children, bad for education, and bad for states' long-term economic prosperity. Many states were in effect lying to students and parents, telling them that students were ready for careers and college when they were nowhere near ready....On K-12 education, our theory of action starts with the four assurances incorporated in last year's economic stimulus bill, the American Recovery and Reinvestment Act. The four assurances got their name from the requirement that each governor in the 50 states had to provide an 'assurance' they would pursue reforms in these four areas--in exchange for their share of funds from a Recovery Act [ARRA- 2009-2012] program designed to largely stem job loss among teachers and principals...The Obama administration has sought to fundamentally shift the federal role, so that the Department is doing much more to support reform and innovation in states, districts, and local communities" (Duncan 2013).

This speech is a mixture of good information and lies. Duncan provides clarity on the purpose of the data systems that states are mandated to adopt, namely, to TRACK citizens for the rest of their lives. His speech also clarifies the fact that the federal government has thrown our states under the bus, also good to know. "...many states had dummied down academic standards to make students look proficient," when in reality, the states standards met or exceeded the Common Core State Standards. Duncan's discussion of the 50 states providing "assurances" that they would pursue reform, however, is a lie, for they were forced to adopt the Common Core standards or lose substantial funding, a point he eloquently glossed over in his speech. One final point I would like to draw your attention to is the federal government's pursuit of weakening state sovereignty and transferring more power to the executive branch of government. Duncan referred to this goal again in 2012 when he stated "...We have tried to flip the traditional tight-loose relationship between the federal government and the states, where the federal government has been loose..." (C.

Swasey 2013). The Obama administration admits openly that they are intentionally violating not only the 10th Amendment which clearly places the majority of governing power in the hands of the states and their citizens, but also the General Educational Provisions Act (GEPA law) that clearly states that the Department of Education has no authority.

The Conservative Teachers of American organization wrote their response to the Common Core State Standards Initiative in a 2012 article entitled: "Common Core Standards and the Federalization of Education" (Schroeder 2012). "Common Core Standards and the Federalization of Education" contains a solid discussion of the road to universal education, and it further states "Many are concerned that the Common Core Standards, once successfully implemented, will provide unfettered access of our educational system by the United Nations. Some textbooks and curricula for our public schools have already been written by the [United Nations Educational, Scientific, and Cultural Organization] UNESCO and the International Baccalaureate program, that is currently in many school districts, across the United States. Grabbing additional access is a natural next step. Once they write the curricula, they must have authority to develop all testing tools. They will decide who becomes a teacher and what preparation will be provided for that teacher. The International Baccalaureate curriculum upsets parents and teachers because the focus includes sustainable development, abortion rights, gay marriage, universal disarmament and social justice curricula…The UN involvement in the American educational system has already been facilitated by treaties signed by American presidents from both parties. Those documents include but are not limited to: Universal Declaration of Human Rights, Treaty on the Rights of the Child, Civic Education: Classroom Connections, and Agenda 21."

The International Baccalaureate program (IB) that the article refers to is another program in which the US partnered with the UN to bring global education to American classrooms, an elite precursor to the Common Core State Standards. The IB is a nonprofit organization that is aligned with the UN's Millennial Goals and works with schools, governments, and international organizations to develop "challenging programs of international education and rigorous assessment," and is known for being the school of choice for the children of American Diplomats and corporate executives. In recent years, however, the IB program has broadened its horizons into the typical American public school, including some that are inner city. There are currently over 1,600 IB schools in the US. The IB program fully endorses the Common Core program.

The IB program was created in Switzerland on the premise that it would help create more compassionate citizens, and that world citizenship needs to begin early in life for the full development of understanding and appreciating the diverse nature of one's own culture. The new understanding of American culture has been a blatant rewriting of history — one that belittles the values that encourage Americans to dream and to achieve those dreams. Remember, the IB program was not developed in America. The philosophy of the IB program is centered on collectivism, one world values and attitudes, de-emphasizing loyalty to nationality and a requirement that IB schools to support UNESCO's agenda. The program has been compared to accelerated programs such as the College Board's Advance Placement program, and is slated to continue in that capacity for the future, with Common Core being the program for the "average" student. Those students who move faster through the standards will be the 20% selected for higher education, the global children selected for Advanced Placement, otherwise known as International Baccalaureate, having the "right attitudes" (Caroline Porter 2013).

Duncan Koler, author of the article "Research Shows True Agenda of IB Program," notes the correlation between the UN's goals and the goals of the IB program (Koler 2012), which have that familiar language contained in Common Core literature: "The U.N. says: (1) we need to downplay nationality in teaching, lest the kids identify too strongly with their country (this was written about in the 1948 UNESCO handbook, "Is There a Way of Teaching for Peace?"); (2) we need to teach "peace" defined by the U.N. as social equity (redistribution of resources); (3) we need to teach "sustainable development" (meaning putting resources out of reach and redistributing others under the guise of environmentalism and social equity); (4) we need to teach local-to-global activism to our kids; and (5) the U.N.'s related Non-Governmental Organizations (called "NGO's) - including IBO, are legally bound to execute UNESCO's educational objectives and to report back to UNESCO on their activities and results."

In Expanding Student Access to a Rigorous International Education: An IB Position Paper on the Common Core State Standards CCSS the IB program states its support of the Common Core Standards: "The IB is pleased to have been selected in 2011 as one of 5 sets of standards against which the Common Core was measured by education experts to determine its success in meeting its goals. The IB recognizes that the implementation of the CCSS will have a significant impact on public schools in states that adopt the new standards. The IB is committed to supporting schools with a range of services and academic tools as outlined in this statement" (International Baccalaureate Organization 2011).

IB goes on to say in the section of the position paper, Meeting the Expectations of the Common Core, that "IB schools and students are well positioned to incorporate the principles of the CCSS into existing IB frameworks. The IB is committed to supporting schools with implementation of the new standards. The framework for delivery of all IB programs, the teaching practices, and the added curricular content of the DP courses provide a proven model for schools in meeting CCSS standards. IB assessment practices provide a model for varied, authentic, relevant tasks that measure student success against cognitive skills learned. The IB supports teachers by providing (required) professional development courses which expand teacher's knowledge and skill in leading students to success. IB standards and practices for schools, teachers and administrators create an entire pedagogical framework to maximize student learning and growth. Many- if not all- CCSS standards are in practice in authorized IB schools."

International Baccalaureate and Common Core State Standards share the mission to create a global community. CCSS and IB focus on changing the social and political views of students altering the intended purpose of educating children. InBloom would be proud.

STANDARDIZED ASSESSMENT

"Passing tests doesn't begin to compare with inquiring, searching, pursuing topics that engage us and excite us. In fact, you will remember what you discover - if you pursue this kind of learning.." - Noam Chomsky

FAQ: Will common assessments be developed? "Two consortia of states are developing common assessments – the Partnership for Assessment of Readiness for College and Career (PARCC) and the Smarter Balanced Assessment Consortium (SBAC). These state-led consortia on assessment are grounded in the following principles: Allow for comparison across students, schools, districts, states and nations; Create economies of scale; Provide information and support more effective teaching and learning; and Prepare students for college and careers (Achieve, Common Core State Standards Initiative 2012).

Merriam-Webster defines "assess" as this:
to make a judgment about (something);
to officially say what the amount, value, or rate of (something) is;
to tax or charge (someone or something) : to require (a person, business, etc.) to pay a particular amount of money (Encylopedia Brittanica, Merriam-Webster Unknown)

In her book "The Deliberate Dumbing Down of America," Charlotte Iserbyt discusses assessments, defining the process as "an estimation; determination of the significance or value of. As used in education, a general term for measuring student progress. Conflict in definition occurs when considering that this is a measurement process used to determine the value or significance of a particular outcome in educational performance. Therefore, it is not a true measurement, but a process of assigning value to specific tasks, creating a cumulative score for performance instead of an accurate measurement against a standard."

The Department of Education and advocates of standardized assessments claim that student achievement has been flat for the past two decades. Diane Ravitch, however, presents the actual evidence in her latest book, Reign of Error, that says otherwise. The data shows that there have been noteworthy increases in reading and mathematics since, more so in mathematics. Diane Ravitch further notes "Reading scores in fourth grade have improved slowly, steadily, and significantly since 1992 for almost every group of students" and includes the data to back it up. The proportion of students who were proficient increased, and the proportion of students who were below basic decreased. This data includes African-American and Hispanic-American students. American Indians were the only group who had a decline in proficiency, and the existence and impact of influencing factors in this situation are not measured or recorded by standardized assessments (Ravitch, Reign of Error 2013).

Standardized testing made headlines in 1994 when the first results of the National Assessment of Educational Progress (NAEP) were published. NAEP aggregated data from 1970 to 1994 from tests given to students aged 9, 13 and 17. As Kris Nielson discusses in his book, Children of the Core, the results revealed predicable information about gaps in achievement for African-American and Hispanic-American children. It is interesting to note that 98% of the students testing proficient were not participating in the Title 1 program, yet only 2% of the students who were participating in Title 1 were proficient. Nelson also notes that the NAEP discloses that the assessment results should not be considered an indicator of the success or failure of the Title 1 program, for there are a number of influencing factors involved that the assessments do not measure (Nielsen 2013).

NCLB took the assessment program further by implementing punitive measures based on assessment information, and rewards if schools attained 100% proficiency in the subjects assessed by 2014. The goals were so high, however, that they were virtually unattainable, so much so, that the practice of dumbing down the definition of proficiency, as well as the diversion from substantial content that standardized testing is too narrow to include became a means of increasing the chances of higher scores. In addition, NCLB narrowly focused on math and reading, completely leaving out other meaningful subjects such as civics, history, literature, science and art. It hollowed out the meaningful depth of education, replacing it with a focus on basic skills in reading and math that required teaching to follow the test (Sacks 1999). Higher test scores with lots of data was the goal, not education, shifting teaching time from balanced to heavy on reading and math, lacking in everything else (Ravitch, The Death and Life of the Great American School System 2010). NCLB's premise was that the assessments were designed to measure student learning, as opposed to the Common Core assessments, which shift the focus to measuring educators' teaching. Standardized assessments, however, do neither. What did thrive as a result of the movement toward standardized testing, with its measure and punish mentality, were tutoring, test preparatory materials and services, as well as testing services.

Common Core's two testing consortia's are developing two different approaches to standardized assessment. Smarter Balanced is developing a "computer-adaptive test," which means the next question depends upon how the student answered the previous question. Correctly-answered questions will generate a more difficult one next, while a question answered incorrectly will generate an easier question following it. The questions are largely open-ended and will be graded by a computer.

PARCC, however, is designing an assessment that draws from a bank of questions for each grade level. Unlike the Smarter Balanced assessment, students at a particular grade level will receive similar questions regardless of performance on previous questions. On the assessment, students are often asked to do more than choose the right answer. Many questions require written justifications or the selection of multiple correct answers from a list. Both tests are said to emphasize "context, rigor and synthesis" (Swanson 2013).

One challenge with the new standardized testing is the fact that they will be administered on the computer. This year, typing skills are being practiced for the first time in the elementary grades. I will not argue that reasonable skills on a keyboard are a worthwhile skill; however, learning them to take a test is more teaching to the test, and I take issue with the continued whittling away of valuable time engaged in meaningful educational activities.

In addition, computers and the one-dimensional world it presents pose a problem with a number of children with learning disabilities, and I, incidentally, have the same issue. Let me explain. I have ADHD, and I struggle with comprehension when reading many texts online; consequently, I print a lot of material, and the shift from one dimensional to two dimensional allows my brain to interact with it differently. The fact that I can makes notes, highlight and flip back and forth between pages eliminates comprehension difficulties. My issues are common, particularly with children who have ADHD, dyslexia or Autism. How many students did I just describe? Yet, not only is standardized testing all on the computer, but Obama already announced he wants all textbooks gone and everything electronic. By the way, I also have a tendency to not do well on standardized testing, such as the ACT, but was identified gifted early on. You would never be able to tell that from a standardized assessment.

According to the federal government, the tests are designed "to encourage higher-level thinking." For instance, instead of a typical multiple choice test, students will respond to questions in essay form, "reflecting" on their answers, moving from simply memorizing basic facts and spitting them back out on a test. This approach will "make learning meaningful and encourage students to be lifelong learners, not robots built to remember facts one day only to forget them the next" (Achieve, Common Core State Standards Initiative 2012). Standardized testing, however, does not capture rich data that truly reflects a child's capabilities. They can test all they want, and the results will never reflect the complete picture that a child's life paints.

Think about that for a moment. Again, we read a purposeful selection of words that sell, and these concepts could be more appropriate for older students; however, the tests have already proven to be convoluted and so poorly written that highly educated adults aren't able to pass it. In March of 2013, 60% of well-educated and accomplished adults who took the Common Core standardized assessment for high school graduation "bombed." As one junior at Hope High School in Providence stated, "Of course it is true that many of these professionals who participated in our event had not been prepared to take the test. But our point is, neither have we. For 10, 11, or 12, years, we have been taught to different standards. We have not been following a curriculum aligned with this test, and we are trapped in an education system that is failing to give us the education we deserve. If it does not make sense to punish adults for not being prepared to take this particular test, we believe it does not make sense to punish us for not having been effectively taught this material over a period of years. Give us a good education, not a test" (Strauss, 60% of Adults Who Took Standardized Test Bombed 2013).

A school board member who took the tests as the Florida Comprehensive Assessment Test, summed up his experience in an email: "I won't beat around the bush…The math section had 60 questions. I knew the answers to none of them, but managed to guess ten out of the 60 correctly. On the reading test, I got 62%. In our system, that's a "D", and would get me a mandatory assignment to a double block of reading instruction … It seems to me something is seriously wrong. I have a bachelor of science degree, two masters degrees, and 15 credit hours toward a doctorate If I'd been required to take those two tests when I was a 10th grader, my life would almost certainly have been very different. I'd have been told I wasn't 'college material,' would probably have believed it, and looked for work appropriate for the level of ability that the test said I had … It makes no sense to me that a test with the potential for shaping a student's entire future has so little apparent relevance to adult, real-world functioning. Who decided the kind of questions and their level of difficulty? Using what criteria? To whom did they have to defend their decisions? As subject-matter specialists, how qualified were they to make general judgments about the needs of this state's children in a future they can't possibly predict? Who set the pass-fail 'cut score'? How? … I can't escape the conclusion that decisions about the [state test] in particular and standardized tests in general are being made by individuals who lack perspective and aren't really accountable" (V. Strauss 2011).

The tests were designed to create failure. The same corporations who design the tests, who know exactly which questions are hard, easy, or somewhere in the middle, and what proportion of students will fail or pass, design tests to produce the results that they want. The more poor results on standardized tests, the more teachers they can replace with their own assembly-line Teach for America prototypes, and the more schools they can close to be reopened as charter schools. Manipulation and misrepresentation with a capital "M".

Standardized tests do not measure creativity, imagination, curiosity, relationship building, value of fellow humans, appreciation of and ability in the arts; initiative, effort, irony, affective judgment, commitment, nuance, good will, humor, compassion, fairness, ethical reflection, . Even at their best, standardized tests measure isolated skills and facts, no matter how creative you get with the wording or mode of responding. In addition, standardizing assessments ignores a plethora of relevant factors, such as disabilities; emotional state of the child that day; the type of community the child lives in; parents' education; physical health of the child that day; special health concerns that affect learning and/or testing; poverty rate; cultural factors; age; life experiences; resources available; learning style; and test anxiety (Kohn 2000).

I ran across a Pearson blog that asks "How do you know your child is learning?" with the caption under it that reads "Testing is one important way for parents and teachers to monitor a child's progress in school" (Pearson, Inc, 2013). Not only do we know this is a blatant lie, but in fifteen minutes, a teacher or a parent can ascertain exactly where a child is in a number of subjects, including reading level and math capabilities, without technology. A child's portfolio with work examples is much "richer," accurate, and useful information than the standardized tests the government has inundated us with over the past several decades. When I worked for the Wyoming Department of Education, this was a major complaint about progress monitoring requirements, which meant more expensive tests like Dibels that had to be administered several times a year, along with the other mandatory testing, and that are unnecessary, and even largely useless, for gauging a student's progress, strengths and weaknesses. Politics has diverted so much of our teachers' time and schools' resources away from education and to jumping through hoops it really is no wonder that many of our students are struggling. Teachers are not allowed to teach anymore—it's all about the test and data.

Dr. Richard Vieille, a clinical psychologist in California who works primarily with adolescents and young adults, notes that anxiety levels for teens is "through the roof." "High stakes tests put an enormous amount of sustained pressure on administrators and teachers, which then trickles down to students and their families," says Dr. Stephanie Roberts, an instructor for school counseling at Texas State University. Everyone knows the stakes involved, from opportunities for students in the future to teachers being able to keep their jobs and schools staying open (McGowan 2013). Long-term stress, like that produced by high-stakes standardized testing, creates a sustained exposure of the brain to the stress hormone, cortisol, which in turn damages the brain. Students are the ultimate performers on the tests, and they are well aware that the results of their answers impacts everyone else involved in education. That's a tremendous burden to place on a child's shoulders.

In an article about standardized testing I read recently, a Chicago mom had this to say: "Year after year, I have watched my child stress over testing. Year after year, the stakes have only gotten higher and the intense pressure to attain the magic score continue to grow." Chicago Teachers Union Spokeswoman Karen Lewis announced recently that they were calling for the cessation of standardized assessment of children in the lower grades and a reduction of testing of students in other grades, saying ""We object to the growing trend to mandate unproven standardized tests which are a major drain on classroom time, undermine education and stand in stark contrast to the proven student assessment tools of classroom teacher developed quizzes, exams, checklists and homework." Chicago Public Schools CEO Barbara Byrd-Bennett announced that the state backs this decision: "As a former teacher and principal, I felt that our parents and educators raised valid concerns around district-wide testing, and our collective work has resulted in 15 fewer tests this school year, adding valuable learning time to the school day to help ensure that every child graduates 100 percent college-ready and 100 percent college-bound (Schlikerman 2013).

For children in the lower elementary grades of kindergarten through second grade, standardized testing poses a unique set of challenges. Students suppress anxiety at young ages, which later manifests as apathy and disengagement as they grow older. In addition, younger children have much shorter attention spans, and the chances of obtaining usable data from test response are slim (Solley 2007).

New York was the first state to administer the new standardized assessments to its students. Less than one-third scored well enough to meet the standards (Simpson 2013). In addition, the New York results classified 40% of Syracuse' teachers as needing improvement plans because they scored below "effective" on their state-mandated performance evaluations, which uses the student test scores as a heavy indicator of teacher effectiveness, according to preliminary results released by the district (Riede 2013).

We have lost, and will continue to lose, a high number of amazing teachers with priceless experience who are dedicated to our students. They will be replaced, as some already have, by younger, inexperienced, poorly educated and lower paid teachers who are easily manipulated.

I recently became aware of Pearson's practice of using temporary employees who were paid $12 an hour and hired from Craigslist to score the essay portions of standardized tests under NCLB (V. Strauss, Pearson Criticized for Finding Test Essay Scorers on Craigslist 2013). While Pearson's ad for the position stated that a bachelor's degree was required, Dan Rather Reports discovered in 2011 that the majority of those hired had not graduated from high school (Carey 2011). Many admitted to making scores up, or rescoring tests to meet a daily goal. In addition, Todd Farley, who spent years in the standardized test scoring industry, not only corroborates Dan Rather's findings in his book Making the Grade, but details a number of other horror stories as well. For instance, the financial penalties for scorers who did not meet the impossibly-high daily quota of tests scored were so punitive that scorers "cut whatever corners we could to get it done." Farley is in constant contact with friends and colleagues in the testing industry today, and is privy to current events and information. One source in the industry recently commented to him that "the testing industry is worse than porn…I feel so dirty" (Farley 2011). Yet, the futures of students, teachers and schools hinges on standardized testing.

A parent, teacher and school board member in Voluntown, Connecticut commented recently on the new standardized tests: "As an example of the Common Core approach to language arts…a multiple-choice question might have more than one answer. There might be five right answers out of eight. That means a different way of testing…Kids have to have a deeper level of comprehension [and confusion] than in the past. Kids are having to be readers certainly beyond what I did [when I was] in school" (Steinhagan 2013). So, Common Core defines "rigor" as creating confusions on standardized assessments? Then it throws in unqualified scorers who admit to providing inaccurate test scores for personal gain, so that the information that is produced is unreliable, unfairly penalizes students, teachers and schools, profoundly impacts lives, wastes untold amounts of time and money, and we are supposed to quietly comply? Not this mom!

Colorado will begin implementing the new standardized tests next year. In the meantime, the state is using the same testing system that produced the results described above. As a result, my daughter will not take another standardized test. In other words, I am opting her out—refusing the test.

Refusing the test, you say? Yes…refusing, as in, formally choose, as is your parental right, to have your child NOT take standardized assessments. Refusing standardized testing protects our children and our teachers, and it sends a respectful message that forcing children to engage non-evidence-based and harmful testing is simply not going to be tolerated. The federal government is confused: we are not accountable to them, they are accountable to us.

How do I refuse standardized testing?

Well, I'm not going to tell you.

Somebody else can do it better.

United Opt Out National at http://unitedoptout.com/ is a one-stop, comprehensive, extremely informative, user-friendly, and useful site that answers this question completely, step by step. United Opt Out provides state-specific opt out guides, as well as tools and resources such as sample opt out letters, talking points, potential difficulties and how to handle them. Dr. Tim Slekar, one of the founders of United Opt Out National and a parent who has opted his own son out of high-stakes-testing, is frustrated with how high-stakes-tests are being misused, subsequently harming our teachers and our children: "…all of this testing, test prep homework, data driven instruction and holding teachers accountable has sent an entire generation of students to careers and college less prepared to do real intellectual work and lacking any sense of imagination and curiosity. This system is destroying our children." He firmly believes that opting out is "the only thing we have that has a chance at stopping this insanity" and that this "decision is pro child, pro teacher and pro public school." Dr. Slekar give us a profound reminder: "Taking care of our children is our first responsibility. … We are talking about stopping the intellectual abuse and demeaning educational experiences our children have had to sit through for 10 years" (Slekar 2012).

So, please put the book down and pull up the site for United Opt Out. Seriously. Spend some time on it—please…now—you can finish reading this book tomorrow. Please. Refusing standardized testing is a critical step in protecting our kids and stopping the Common Core monster.

Data Collection and Privacy: Who, What and Why

"I know no safe depositor of the ultimate powers of society but the people themselves; and if we think them not enlightened enough to exercise their control with wholesome discretion, the remedy is not to take it from them but to inform their discretion." ~ Thomas Jefferson, 1820

FAQ: Are there data collection requirements associated with the Common Core State Standards? There are no data collection requirements of states adopting the CCSS. Standards define expectations for what students should know and be able to do by the end of each grade. Implementing the CCSS does not require data collection. The means of assessing students and the data that results from those assessments are up to the discretion of each state and are separate and unique from the CCSS (Achieve, Common Core State Standards Initiative 2012).

I usually try to give people the benefit of the doubt in situations when inaccurate information is given, but I think by now it is clear that the federal government and corporate advocates of the Common Core State Standards Initiative lie…a lot.

The much-talked about longitudinal data collection system, is a comprehensive database compiled on each child, and if Arne Duncan, Bill Gates and the rest of the Common Core hoodlums have their way, from conception to burial. This data is not aggregate data, meaning it is generic identifiable by data piece. Oh, no… it is linked specifically to the child, personally identifiable (Kaplan 2013). Data that is collected will follow the child through to their adult years and beyond. In fact, that is the purpose of the SLDS, to provide a database that "grows" along with the child into their career years.

The creators of the Common Core were very clear in stating that the success of the standards balances on the creation of an extensive data base. The seeds of this were planted in 2002 with the Education Science Reform Act that gave the federal government the authority to publish guidelines for states developing state longitudinal data systems (SLDS). Since then, the federal government has created a host of incentives and federally funded data models have spurred encouraged states to monitor students' early years, performance in college, and success in the workforce by following "individuals systematically and efficiently across state lines" (Dodrill 2013).

The Department of Education added bricks to this concept by altering the Family Educational Rights and Privacy Act (FERPA) outside the parameters of the legislative process for amending federal statute. FERPA formerly guaranteed that parents could access their children's personally identifiable information collected by schools, but schools were barred from sharing this information with third parties. FERPA defines personally identifiable information as information "that would allow a reasonable person in the school community, who does not have personal knowledge of the relevant circumstances, to identify the student with reasonable certainty," including names of family members, living address, Social Security number, date and place of birth, disciplinary record, and biometric record (C. Swasey, Without Authority: The Federal Access of Private Data Using Common Core 2013). However, the Department of Education has reshaped FERPA through regulations so that any government or private entity that the department says is evaluating an education program has access to students' personally identifiable information. Postsecondary institutes and workforce education programs can also be given this data. This regulatory change absent congressional legislation has resulted in a lawsuit against the Department of Education.

"Personally Identifiable Information" will be extracted from each student, which will include the following data: parents' names, address, Social Security Number, date of birth, place of birth, mother's maiden name, etc. On the other hand, according to the SLDS brief, "Sensitive Information" will also be extracted, which delves into the intimate details of students' lives:

1. Political affiliations or beliefs of the student or parent;

2. Mental and psychological problems of the student or the student's family;

3. Sex behavior or attitudes;

4. Illegal, anti-social, self-incriminating, and demeaning behavior;

5. Critical appraisals of other individuals with whom respondents have close family relationships;

6. Legally recognized privileged or analogous relationships, such as those of lawyers, physicians, and ministers;

7. How many bedrooms are in the home and who sleeps in each one;

8. Religious practices, affiliations, or beliefs of the student or the student's parent; or

9. Income (other than that required by law to determine eligibility for participation in a program or for receiving financial assistance under such program)

Students' personal information will be submitted to a database managed by InBloom, Inc., a private organization funded largely by the Bill and Melinda Gates Foundation. The fact that Common Core Standards require children's personal information to be provided to a database that can be expected to sell or share the data to unspecified companies is worrisome to many parents and educators. "It leads to total control and total tracking of the child," said Mary Black, curriculum director for Freedom Project Education, an organization that provides classical K-12 online schooling. "It completely strips the child of his or her own privacy" (Cook 2013). At this time there are four hundred points of data slated to collected, monitored and stored on every child in the American education system. Monitoring devices are being implemented in our children's classrooms. All of this is being done under the guise of education reform.

In 1990, the Secretary of Labor appointed a commission to determine the skills our young people need to succeed in the world of work. The commission's purpose was to encourage a high-performance economy characterized by highly skilled, high earning workforce. The commission completed its work in 1992, and its findings and recommendations continue to be used in a multitude of improvement efforts, most recently, education (Evaluation and Training Administration 2011). The purpose of the Five-Year Research and Evaluation Strategic Plan for 2012-2017 was to identify high priority topic areas to be used in planning research and evaluation efforts through 2012. Under Section 171 of the Workforce Investment Act of 1998 (WIA), after consultation with States, localities, and other stakeholders, the Secretary of Labor was to prepare a plan that describes "demonstration and pilot, multi-service, research, and multistate projects that focus on employment and training priorities for the five-year period following the plan. The plan is to contain strategies to address national employment and training problems and take into account factors such as the availability of existing research; the need to ensure results that have interstate validity; the benefits of economies of scale and the efficiency of proposed projects; and the likelihood that the results of the projects will be useful to policymakers and stakeholders in addressing employment and training problems." Examples of this in action are the Common Core Standards State Initiative and economic improvement efforts in Nevada, where Governor Sandoval of Nevada was named Vice Chair of the National Governor's Association Education and Workforce Committee in October. Members of the committee are to ensure that the governors' views are represented in the shaping of federal policy. "Education and workforce development are a constant priority for all governors. I look forward to working on education policies affecting our great state," states Sandoval.

The Workforce Data Quality Initiative's Mission Statement from the United States Department of Labor's website reads:

"The long-term Workforce Data Quality Initiative and SLDS goal for States is to use their longitudinal data systems to follow individuals through school and into and through their work life...Enable workforce data to be matched with education data to ultimately create longitudinal data systems with individual-level information beginning with pre-kindergarten through post-secondary schooling all the way through entry and sustained participation in the workforce and employment services system (Labor 2012).

The SLDS has been implemented nationwide in each state. It became fully operational in 2012.

Along the way the SLDS was transformed into the P20W, or the Preschool through age 20 Workforce Tracking. As the US Department of Labor stated, the P20W is to "enable workforce data to match with education data...with individual-level information." It is a "cradle to career" monitoring system. Children will not be the only ones under scrutiny. Teachers are going to be linked directly to their students and their performance will be assessed on the data that is collected. Parents' information is also being collected. This is essentially a complete dossier on every American that will follow them throughout their life. A permanent record of their beliefs, behavior, and their preferences.

How is this possible if we have privacy laws in place specifically for the handling of personal information? With the implementation of the SLDS, the FERPA (Family Education Rights and Privacy Act) had to be altered, and the Constitution, as well as a number of federal laws had to be ignored. In December of 2011 FERPA was amended, outside the legal parameters to amend anything federal, to include exceptions in which student information could be shared without parental knowledge or consent (Clark 2013).

Let's take a look at the exception. "One exception, which permits disclosure without consent, is disclosure to school officials with legitimate educational interests. A school official is a person employed by the school as an administrator, supervisor, instructor, or support staff member (including health or medical staff and law enforcement unit personnel) or a person serving on the school board. A school official may also include a volunteer or contractor outside of school who performs an institutional service of function for which the school would otherwise use its own employees and who is under the direct control of the school with respect to the use and maintenance of PII from education records such as an attorney, auditor, medical consultant, or therapist; a parent or student volunteering to serve on an official committee, such as a disciplinary or grievance committee; or parent, student, or other volunteer assisting another school official in performing his or her tasks. A school official has a legitimate educational interest if the official needs to review an education record in order to fulfill his or her professional responsibility" (US Department of Education 2012). Did we leave anyone out? Basically anyone, anywhere, for any reason can access your child's information without your knowledge or consent.

"The sector is undeniably hot; technology startups aimed at K-12 schools attracted more than $425 million in venture capital last year, according to the NewSchools Venture Fund, a nonprofit that focuses on the sector. The investment company GSV Advisors tracked 84 deals in the sector last year, up from 15 in 2007. In addition to its $100 million investment in the database, the Gates Foundation has pledged $70 million in grants to schools and companies to develop personalized learning tools" (Logue 2013). After discovering all of this, I took a firsthand look at the P20 Longitudinal Data System—Student Data Points, and I completely blown away at the enormity of the list before me.

Common Core proponents state there is no data collection laid out in the standards. They defend themselves by staying, "they are only standards." But the standards allow for common coded data sets to compare children. Achieve's website states "States must collect, coordinate, and use K-12 and postsecondary data to track and improve the readiness of graduates to succeed in college and the workplace" (Bean 2013). If there were not "common" standards and assessments, then the tracking of children via a common data set would not be possible. Common Core provides the framework for common "direct child assessments," and publishes it all in the Federal Register.

The National Education Data Model (NEDM) outlines over 400 data points that CCSS proponents say will never be used (Data Quality Campaign 2013). However, this data and more will be gathered from parents, teachers, school administrators and non-parental care providers, including, but NOT limited to (InBloom 2012):

•Residence after exiting or withdrawing from school

82

•School id from which transferred

•Activity code

•Activity involvement beginning date

•Additional post-school accomplishments

•At-risk status

•Base salary or wage

•Additional special health needs, information, or instructions

•Apartment, room, suite number

•Assignment type

•Assignment finish date

•Building/site number

•Bus stop arrival time

•Bus stop to school distance

•Community Service hours

•Employment permit description

•Employment permit number

•Family Income Range

•Family Public Assistance Status

•Health Care History Episode Date

•Injury description

•Length of Placement in neglected or delinquent program

•Neglected or delinquent progress level

•Preparing for nontraditional fields status

•Score interpretation information

•Tribal or clan name

•Uniform Resource Identifier

•Unsafe School Choice status
FCAT Scans—in the Dept of Education's own paperwork

•Biomeasuring devices, including fingerprint scanners

In addition, facial recognition cameras will be mounted on computers, and will enable teachers and administrators, and goodness knows who else, to evaluate our children's emotional responses to what they are learning or to what is said to them. A pressure sensitive mouse will enable evaluators to measure stress when our children are required to do something. A posture-sensitive chair will reveal temperament via body language. Health monitoring bracelets are also being implemented in schools throughout the nation. These devices are a pedometer and heart rate monitor all-in-one. Children are being encouraged to wear these at school, and even in some instances, at home as well. This is directly from the Promoting Grit, Tenacity and Perseverance document from the Department of Education, page 44, which even comes complete with pictures (US Dept of Education 2013).

The second method of collection is through data mining hidden in the assessments. Here is a small sample:

In this section, please tell us about yourself and your family.

1. Which of the following best describes you? Fill in one or more ovals. White, Black or African American, Asian, American Indian or Alaska Native,   Native Hawaiian or other Pacific Islander.

2. Do you have the following in your home? Fill in ovals for all that apply: Access to the Internet, clothes dryer just for your family, dishwasher, more than one bathroom, your own bedroom.

3. How often do people in your home talk to each other in a language other than English?

4. Do the following people live in your home? Fill in ovals for all that apply. Mother, stepmother, foster mother or other female legal guardian, father, stepfather, foster father or other male legal guardian.

What bearing on our children's knowledge of Mathematics and Reading does their ethnicity, appliance ownership status, and family dynamic have? An adult would have the right to not answer these invasive and pointless questions. A child doesn't know they can decline. It is part of the test. Are they not taught to answer all of the questions on the test?

The end purpose is to be able to inventory and monitor the human capital, our children. Major corporations have invested a lot of money in education and they are expecting a return on that investment. Not only are they expecting a monetary gain, but they are also counting on a guaranteed future workforce specifically trained to meet their corporate needs.

Our children are more than a guaranteed future workforce. They have hopes, dreams and desires that they should be allowed to fulfill without the government dictating to them what they can or cannot do.

Common Core Standards and Child Development

"Every child in America entering school at the age of five is insane because he comes to school with certain allegiances to our founding fathers, toward our elected officials, toward his parents, toward a belief in a supernatural being, and toward the sovereignty of this nation as a separate entity. It's up to you as teachers to make all these sick children well – by creating the international child of the future." -Dr. Chester M. Pierce.

The International Child Defined in 1973. Is This the Reason for the Increased Push for Universal Preschool?

Here is a story I caught on Facebook recently from a mom with a kindergartner: "My husband and I sat down with my daughter's teacher yesterday for a parent - teacher conference. I must say that we couldn't have asked for a better teacher for her but as we discussed her progress so far, she informed me that our daughter was in the 'needs improvement' column because she couldn't write three sentences that built upon each other. She needed a beginning, middle and end to go along with the three pictures she drew. She told the teacher the story orally, but was unable to write the sentences without direct assistance. Since she couldn't do it on her own, she was marked as unsatisfactory. Now she has a personal education plan to help her "grow enough" to pass the next, even harder test. She is a kindergartener. This is week 10. This is Common Core State Standards in action. This is wrong."

Children who enter kindergarten developmentally are not ready to write stories, much less critique their classmates' work, which Common Core prescribes for all grades. The average kindergartener is six years old, just learning to tie shoes, button jackets and interacting with others in a personal way. Many may already know the alphabet and numbers. They start learning reading and writing their names at this age, with some simple math concepts. I remember learning sets and subsets at this age. Do they even teach that anymore? Children this age developmentally are not capable yet of reflecting introspectively upon their own thinking, and asking them to reflect upon and respond, verbally or written, to text is asking them to do something their brains cannot do yet. Asking teachers to present material that children are not developmentally ready for results in hours spent repeating material over and over, leaving little or no time to engage in meaningful activities, like play. Play and exploration are, in essence, young children's work, and is invaluable to their creating understanding of the world around them. Play leads to examination of colors, shapes, cause and effect, social skills, language, music, art…the list goes on for the possibilities are endless. The above example punishes a young child for not doing something they are not able to do. I call this child abuse, and the ensuing stress will permanently damage the brain. Excessive production of the stress hormone cortisol injures the brain, and the psychological ramifications of the ongoing stress and anxiety created by standardized testing driving education are profound. In addition, children will be trained to spit out answers crafted a certain way, with no true learning. Common Core defines school improvement by simply making it harder with no regard to research, evidence-based practices or child development.

The Common Core State Standards Initiative calls for creating education improvement plans for children who do not do well when they are assessed, and a minimum score must be achieved before advancing to the next grade. That means a high number of children will be held back and given remedial instruction that they do not need. How frustrating is that for the students already subjected to these mandates, and how much worse will it be for the others who will be soon? Children will lose confidence and motivation, for what is the point of working towards a goal you simply cannot achieve?

The National Association for the Education of Young Children (NAEYC) recognizes in its position paper Principles of Child Development and Learning That Inform Developmentally Appropriate Practice (NAEYC 2009) that, while there are certain milestones that children typically reach by certain ages, each child is unique, developing at different rates in different areas and requiring differentiated instruction for education to be effective. "Individual variation has at least two dimensions: the inevitable variability around the average or normative course of development and the uniqueness of each person as an individual (Sroufe, Cooper, & DeHart 1992). Each child is a unique person with an individual pattern and timing of growth, as well as individual personality, temperament, learning style, and experiential and family background. All children have their own strengths, needs, and interests; for some children, special learning and developmental needs or abilities are identified. Given the enormous variation among children of the same chronological age, a child's age must be recognized as only a crude index of developmental maturity… Recognition that individual variation is not only to be expected but also valued requires that decisions about curriculum and adults' interactions with children be as individualized as possible. Emphasis on individual appropriateness is not the same as 'individualism.' Rather, this recognition requires that children be considered not solely as members of an age group, expected to perform to a predetermined norm and without adaptation to individual variation of any kind. Having high expectations for all children is important, but rigid expectations of group norms do not reflect what is known about real differences in individual development and learning during the early years. Group-norm expectancy can be especially harmful for children with special learning and developmental needs." Common Core is rigid; there is no flexibility for differentiation and meeting the wide array of individual needs, learning styles and developmental rates that teachers encounter every day in the classroom.

The NAEYC's position on unacceptable practices in the kindergarten classroom makes it clear the placing the burden on the child in forcing him to conform to the curriculum instead of developing a program of instruction with curricula that fits the child is a current practice that has risen because of the increasing performance pressures foisted onto teachers as a result of policy makers. The benefits of play are being replaced with learning strategies that are not developmentally appropriate for this age group. A day of pencil and paper "learning" activities is not productive and frustrates the child. "Too often teachers are told, or they believe, that it is not enough to set the stage for learning by preparing a rich and varied environment and encouraging children to engage in activities which carry their development forward. In too many kindergartens, the core of rich creative experiences with real materials has now been replaced with abstract curriculum materials requiring pencil-and-paper responses. Often these are linked to tightly sequenced and often inappropriate grade-level lists of expected skill acquisition in each of the subject areas. Ironically, children who are ready to learn to read are more likely to advance as far as they are able in an active learning classroom." In addition, the retention practices that Common Core's standardized testing has already demonstrated that retention rates will substantially increase as a result of the assessments, are just as inappropriate. Assessment of a child's characteristics and academic abilities are more effectively measure as a result of teacher observation, checklists, and portfolios of children's work. "Retention policies should be highly suspect given the lack of demonstrated effectiveness and prevalent bias against certain groups of children. The current methodology used in selecting students for retention makes it impossible to predict accurately who will benefit. Pro-retention policies as a strategy for establishing rigorous academic standards are likely to be self-defeating" (NAEYC 2001).

The benefits of early childhood education are no secret. "The goal of early childhood education is not that all children between birth and five years of age attend a similar classroom setting that looks exactly the same. The goal, instead, is to make sure that all children ages birth to five years have regular and consistent opportunities for enriching and engaging activities, regardless of income or family structure. These activities and opportunities should include time for reading, exploring outside, imaginative play, engaging play with adults, engaging play with peers, and participating and experiencing new things" (O 2013). I don't see any of this taken into consideration in the Common Core Standards. Instead, even though no early childhood education or development specialists had anything to do with the writing of the standards, expectations were set out for our youngest students that do not match their development. Greed overrode research, evidence and common sense.

Mental Health Therapist Joan Landes, speaks quite openly on the effects of the emotionally charged material that is inherent in quite a bit of the curricula that claims to be aligned with Common Core, and has a video on Youtube that I recommend you watch (Landis 2013). In it, she discusses the fact that Common Core curriculum continually engages children on an emotional level by consistently using highly-charges language that is designed to manipulate the listener. The language is clearly designed, she says, to illicit a reaction, not cognition, constantly engaging the limbic system (fight or flight) in children where this system is just developed and the capabilities of restraining the limbic system are still developing. Children are consistently fed material that creates anger, competitiveness, jealousy and resentment. These emotional reactions are reinforced over time, and spending this much time in this mode leads to a highly emotional and reactive individual. None of this is healthy, and is, in fact, damaging. In addition, Landes noted that in an extensive review of Common Core curricula for the younger elementary grades, she found no positive emotions represented.

I recently read an article that a teacher in the first grade wrote about her first experience administering a standardized test to her class. She was heartbroken. Her students looked at her, puzzled, stating over and over "We just don't know how to do this." Some cried. They were afraid to not do well. They were scared. And they kept looking to her for help, and even though she did her best to reassure them that it was just a test and that it didn't matter if they didn't know how to do some things, the children sensed the seriousness of situation. They knew they had not done well, and it crushed them. The teacher was devastated by the end of the day, feeling that she had done something awful to her students. But it wasn't her, it was Common Core. I wonder what Arne would have done?

Common Core and Curriculum

"Let me control the textbooks and I will control the state."

-Adolf Hitler

Common Core repeatedly proclaims that it does not tell teachers how or what to teach. In case you have not seen the standards yet, let me share a choice piece with you:

The Standards should be recognized for what they are not as well as what they are. The most important intentional design limitations are as follows:

1. The Standards define what all students are expected to know and be able to do, not how teachers should teach…Furthermore, while the Standards make references to some particular forms of content, including mythology, foundational U.S. documents, and Shakespeare, they do not—indeed, cannot—enumerate all or even most of the content that students should learn. The Standards must therefore be complemented by a well-developed, content-rich curriculum consistent with the expectations laid out in this document.

2. While the Standards focus on what is most essential, they do not describe all that can or should be taught. A great deal is left to the discretion of teachers and curriculum developers…

3. The Standards do not define the nature of advanced work for students who meet the Standards prior to the end of high school…

4. The Standards set grade-specific standards but do not define the intervention methods or materials necessary to support

students who are well below or well above grade-level expectations….

5. It is also beyond the scope of the Standards to define the full range of supports appropriate for English language learners and for students with special needs. At the same time, all students must have the opportunity to learn and meet the same high standards if they are to access the knowledge and skills necessary in their post–high school lives (Achieve, Common Core State Standards Initiative 2012).

This would be great if it were true; however, the standards are quite detailed, and there is not much room left for choice when all is said and done. In addition, the standardized assessments are built directly from the standards, making it necessary for the curriculum to speak to the standards. The assessments do not measure if a child can add, subtract, multiply, and divide whole numbers, decimals and fractions; they measure specific methodology, and the "new math" contains very different methodology, so much so, in fact, that many teachers are completely unfamiliar with it and are engaging in intensive professional development to learn the methodologies, as well as how to teach them. Common Core changed the methodology for mathematics, therefore it changed what and how teachers present material. It also significantly changed all subjects by integrating writing into everything, including art and PE, as well as the types of texts to be used for the English/Language Arts standards. Teachers have to use Common Core curriculum. The double speak is truly astounding. I challenge you to search for curricula that is not aligned with Common Core. It is very difficult to find, and when you do find it, it is most likely because it is pre-Common Core or is one of the few home schooling curricula available that is pure.

And then, there is this gem from Bill Gates from a speech given in 2009 before the National Council of State Legislators: "The standards will tell the teachers what their students are supposed to learn, and the data will tell them whether they're learning it. These two changes will open up options we've never had before." What was that about the standards not telling teachers what they have to teach?

When one is in the habit of lying, it is difficult to keep up with what lies have been told, and eventually the truth starts slipping out. The Fordham Institute's Thomas Meyer recently wrote an article refuting criticism from Peter Cunningham, former secretary of state. In the article he penned, "In fact, there is no Common Core curriculum, radical or otherwise. Words matter. The Times essay, Cunningham says, "…conflates standards, which are agreed-upon expectations for what children should know in certain subjects by certain ages, with curricula, which are the materials and the approaches that teachers use to help kids learn." There is no such thing as a "radical curriculum" because there is no such thing as a common core curriculum.

Another article, written by Chester E Flynn, Jr., senior fellow at Stanford's Hoover Institution, chairman of Hoover's Task Force on K-12 Education, and president of the Thomas B. Fordham Institute, and Kathleen Porter-Magee, Senior Advisor for Policy and Instruction at The College Board and Senior Director at Fordham, inadvertently contradicts Meyer's statement and points directly to the curriculum issues by saying, "In order for standards to have any impact, however, they must change classroom practice. In Common Core states, the shifts that these new expectations demand are based on the best research and information we have about how to boost students' reading comprehension and analysis and thereby prepare them more successfully for college and careers. Whether those shifts will truly transform classroom practice, however, remains to be seen." What takes place in the classroom, and how would you change it? By changing classroom practice, or, in other words, how teachers teach as well as the curriculum, two things the Common Core Standards swear they don't do.

Jay P. Greene talks about this in an article entitled Fordham and CC-Backers Need to Get Their Stories Straight (Greene 2013). In the article, he notes "The National Council on Teacher Quality, with support and praise from the Fordham Institute, are grading teacher training programs on whether 'The program trains teacher candidates to teach reading as prescribed by the Common Core State Standards.' Wait. 'Prescribed?' I thought Common Core didn't prescribe pedagogy. But that was back when I was young and we were dating." You have to dig a little to find it, but the truth is there.

I am going to hammer away for a while at the math standards, because, while there are concerns regarding all subjects, math seems to be the most glaring curriculum issue at this time. My daughter, Miki, started the fourth grade in August, and we've been wrestling with Common Core Math ever since. My daughter, much like many children across the US, is identified as "gifted" with math being a strong subject and one she has always loved. Not this year. Going into the fourth grade this year, Miki was very strong on addition, subtraction, multiplication and division, as well as place value and simple algebraic equations. She handles word problems well, and feedback from parents has included "strong critical thinking skills" as well as reading, including fluency and comprehension, a grade level above. This looks different this year. Let me explain why.

I want to start with the fact that Common Core leaves out memorizing math facts. While my daughter's school did incorporate memorization of addition and subtraction facts into the curriculum, the introduction of Common Core eliminated fact memorization and she did not have the opportunity to work on memorization of multiplication and division facts in the classroom. I work with her at home, in addition to the increased homework we do as a result of the Common Core curriculum. Let me share a brief excerpt from the book The Glass Wall: Why Mathematics

Seems Difficult, written by Frank Smith, who received his Ph.D. from Harvard and is a former professor at the Ontario Institute for Studies in Education, the University of Toronto, the University of Victoria, British Columbia, and the University of the Witwatersrand, South Africa. "Memory, like understanding, is unavoidable in mathematics and everything else. Although mathematics might seem to be a constant process of 'working things out,' the foundation of any kind of mathematical enterprise is memory, and a great deal of learning mathematics involves committing mathematical facts and procedures to memory. Memory eases all of our way through mathematics, and we can't get started without it. The first conventional step is to memorize, in order, the numbers from one to ten. These have to be known. The next step in an individual's mathematical development is usually 'tables' for addition and multiplication. I'm not referring to printed tables with column after column of numbers arranged in a systematic way as a substitute for memorization, but packages of knowledge that must be committed to memory . . . often a little bit at a time. Tables in this sense are simply organized ways of remembering mathematical facts. (he goes on to describe a variety of methods that can be used to help young children remember) Once memorized, these facts become immediately available for use provided the nature and manner of use is understood. A few simple rhymes conceal a detailed blueprint for the foundations of mathematics. . . Many fundamental mathematical and geometrical relationships are woven in the patterns of these tables, when the numbers are read horizontally, vertically, diagonally, or in leaps and bounds. . . " Memorizing facts lays a foundation, and to skip this step creates a distraction for children learning math functions, for now they cannot focus on the function, but must expend significant mental energy trying to solve the basic piece that should be automatic recall as well (Smith 2002).

Common Core Mathematics prior to the fourth grade focuses on regrouping and place value, but does not focus on the actual functions of addition, subtraction, multiplication and division until the fourth grade. For Miki, this is moot because she had different math in previous grades. She could add, subtract, multiply and divide multi-digit numbers well, and also understood what she was doing. As part of Common Core's "deeper...rigorous...robust" and "strengthening critical thinking skills", there are four new methods introduced in the fourth grade for multiplication and division problems, in addition to the traditional, straightforward algorithm, to which they introduce a variation for a sixth option for solving a multiplication equation. The traditional method is referred to as the "shortcut method" and is presented as harder because it does not create understanding. Students are also expected to provided explanations or justification for their answers as part of the "deeper thinking" and "demonstrated understanding...critical thinking" that the standards demand. Common Core material goes so far to say it is evidence-based and easier to understand, which could not be farther from the truth and there IS research and evidence to back that up. If you recall, this, and the fact that the standards are not internationally benchmarked as claimed, are the reasons why James Milgram refused to sign off on the standards.

The alternate methodologies, also referred to in Houghton-Mifflin's Math Expressions book as "areas of rectangles," are the expanded notation method, the place value sections method, the algebraic notation method, and the lattice method, with all using "ungrouping" to base ten and partial products. I'm not going to try to explain them to you, but I will say this: I have spent enough time talking with the parents of the children in my daughter's class to be able to say unequivocally that this is causing confusion and creating no understanding. They all understand the traditional methods and are struggling with the other methods in an attempt to do well on standardized testing. While some students enjoy some of the alternate methods to do for fun, with the exception of the lattice method, they all prefer the traditional method for homework and tests. The traditional methods reflect the way we think about numbers and are the practical methods we use in real life, unless we have a calculator. I am proficient in Common Core math with the exception of the lattice method. I don't understand it, I am not going to try any longer, and I have worked out an agreement with my daughter's teacher that she does not have to do them. Remember, I opted her out of the standardized testing. With no assessment hanging over her head, there is no point in confusing or frustrating her further. She is free to learn without the pressure.

The following is an article voicing an informed opinion about the Common Core math standards, written by a parent, who also happens to have a PhD in engineering:

"I'm a PhD Engineer. Math is a central component of everything I do – if I'm not using directly, I need to understand what is happening. The understanding these people are looking for won't come until the children begin to mature. Teach 'em the basics, and even if they don't "understand" they can cope later. Don't teach them the basics, and the ones who aren't interested in the basics will never learn.

I have a Ph.D. in Physics, and I'll be damned if I can figure out the last steps in the "lattice" method of multiplication. I'm sure if I spent more than 5 minutes, maybe I could, but really . . . this is multiplication we're talking about! That lattice thing is more confusing than anything I have ever seen. The division methods aren't quite as awful; at least they made sense to me rather quickly. Stick with the older, working algorithms, and leave this other nonsense to the educrats.

This is exactly why my children are being home schooled. For example my daughter is now in 7th grade and is being home schooled for the second year now because she was #1 bullied and the school did nothing (thats a different matter all together) and #2 she was so behind in math because nothing was explain to her and when she brought her work home it was "foreign" to us. Now that she is home she has come into her own and is excelling in math because she is learning the basics that should be taught not this new crap that most adults don't understand. I learned math using the basic way and I turned out just fine.

Years ago, I assisted in a fourth-grade classroom using Everyday Mathematics as the curriculum. At first, I was "sold" because it was developed by the University of Chicago and deemed to be "cutting edge." Who wouldn't want such "advanced" learning for their children? In reality, it was a disaster. Students were regularly lost and confused and had not a clue as to how and why they arrived at their answers–if they arrived at them at all. The only students who "got it" were worked with intensely one-on-one and few, if any, had mastery of simple computation by year's end. Since parents hadn't been taught using this method, they were powerless to help at home. Most classroom days were spent watching students boil over in frustration. This type of math instruction does not work in large groups because it is developed by "educational experts" who have not the first clue as to the realities of the classroom environment" (Tuttle 2013).

My sentiments exactly.

In 2005, a group of well-respected, education experts provided a point-by-point refutation of the reform-movement math standards which greatly influenced the development of the Common Core math standards. They addressed the past two decades of mathematics education in kindergarten through high school classrooms that have been dominated by "unsupported pedagogical theories constructed in our schools of education and propagated by the National Council of Teachers of Mathematics (NCTM). Their curricular and pedagogical 'vision' for mathematics education reform, articulated in the two NCTM standards documents (1989 and 2000), has dominated local, state and federal education decision-making and policies, as well as public discussions, and press coverage. But many parents, mathematics experts, and K-12 teachers of mathematics do not share this vision" (Karen Budd, Elizabeth Carson, Barry Garelick, David Klein, R. James Milgram, Ralph A. Raimi, Martha Schwartz, Sandra Stotsky, Vern Williams, and W. Stephen Wilson, New York City HOLD and Mathematically Correct 2005). As you can see, James Milgram and Sandra Stotsky were members of that group, and they provided an excellent evaluation of ten of the biggest claims of Common Core with solid evidentiary resources to validate their responses.

I want to highlight two of the myths that the group responded to because of their prominence in Common Core material today. The first is "Math concepts are best understood and mastered when presented 'in context'; in that way, the underlying math concept will follow automatically," to which the group responded with "Applications are important and story problems make good motivators, but understanding should come from building the math for universal application. When story problems take center stage, the math it leads to is often not practiced or applied widely enough for students to learn how to apply the concept to other problems. [S]olutions of problems ... need to be rounded off with a mathematical discussion of the underlying mathematics. If new tools are fashioned to solve a problem, then these tools have to be put in the proper mathematical perspective. ... Otherwise the curriculum lacks mathematical cohesion."

The second myth I would like to call to your attention is the claim that "Children develop a deeper understanding of mathematics and a greater sense of ownership when they are expected to invent and use their own methods for performing the basic arithmetical operations, rather than study, understand and practice the standard algorithms." The response to this claim directly addresses the lack of value for the traditional long division Common Core espouses: "Children who do not master the standard algorithms begin to have problems as early as algebra I. The snubbing or outright omission of the long division algorithm by NCTM- based curricula can be singularly responsible for the mathematical demise of its students. Long division is a pre-skill that all students must master to automaticity for algebra (polynomial long division), pre-calculus (finding roots and asymptotes), and calculus (e.g., integration of rational functions and Laplace transforms.) Its demand for estimation and computation skills during the procedure develops number sense and facility with the decimal system of notation as no other single arithmetic operation affords." "The standard algorithms" are the traditional methods you and I learned when we were children.

Having said all of that, I am one of the fortunate one who have not had to pull my daughter and home school her in math. I have opted her out of standardized testing, refusing to have her subjected to it, so that pressure is off of her shoulders. In addition, her school was more than willing to work out an arrangement in which I write a note for the problems that are clearly not appropriate for fourth grade math and that I choose to not have Miki do. Let me just add that I have had candid conversations with her teacher and her principal about Common core, and they are aware that I have spent a tremendous amount of time researching this issue. I am not just picking the hard ones; rather, I believe in challenging a child—appropriately. In addition, the problems I opt her out of are the ones that are causing problems in general.

Common Core espouses that education is not about teaching content, but that it's about "the discovery of content," which is another myth that was dealt with by the above-mentioned group. I recently watch an interview took place recently between guests Christel Swasey, co-founder of the blog Common Core: Education Without Representation, David Cox, also a teacher in Utah, Emmett McGroarty of American Principles Project and

Sherena Arrington, a well-known and highly-respected political consultant with the Georgia Public Policy Foundation. I want to note that Christel Swasey have a B.A. degree in English and a M.A. degree in Communications, both from Brigham Young University. In addition she earned her teaching credential at California State University San Bernardino. During the discussion, she noted that "The difference is when student-centered learning takes the place of instruction from a teaching, then you are just playing around in a sand box and nobody is guiding you and… it's just not effective." Sherena Arrington pointed out that the proponents of Common Core want the students to learn to add the tens first, which "…makes mathematics much more difficult." Arrington also discussed the constant proclamations that American students perform poorly on international assessments, stating, "It matters what tests they are talking about. You will hear it said that American students are 32nd in the world on these international tests. [one of the tests] PISA is about process and fuzzy math. TIMMS [the one Common Core advocates don't like to talk about] which is about content knowledge, academic knowledge. We are in the top 10 in the world." I really think Swasey nailed it, however, when she stated "Those who are promoting these new methods are actually trying to promote the tests that will drive the curriculum" (Christel Swasey 2013).

The Common Core Standards integrate ELA skills into every subject possible, from math to PE. In addition, it proudly touts that it shifts from classic reading to informational texts, and the ELA Standards contain a long discussion about text complexity. I agree with the theory of challenging students, in any subject; however, the overarching principle is reasonable and developmentally appropriate for each student. It is also important to incorporate a variety of literature (Achieve, Common Core State Standards Initiative 2012). Recommended reading includes executive orders, song lyrics, segments from a Federal Reserve newsletter, EPA's "Recommended Levels of Insulation" and an executive order on transportation and the environment. Teachers are told NOT to teach the Gettysburg Address with any background material. This is all in the name of better 'workers' in the global economy" (Emmett McGroarty 2013). History is taught, but in the context of literacy, not in the in depth manner necessary to facilitate an examination of historical events, the intent behind historical events such as the drafting of the US Constitution and history's impact on the present and the future. "Historical thinking involves the ability to identify, describe and evaluate evidence about the past from diverse sources (including written documents, works of art, archaeological artifacts, oral traditions and other primary sources), with respect to content, authorship, purpose, format and audience. It involves the capacity to extract useful information, make supportable inferences and draw appropriate conclusions from historical evidence while also understanding such evidence in its context, recognizing its limitations and assessing the points of view that it reflects." Instead, history is presented in text only, and examination is encouraged in a literal sense. An example is the presentation of Lincoln's Gettysburg Address and questions such as "What does Lincoln mean when he uses the phrase 'four score and seven years ago'?" or "What if Lincoln had used the verb 'start' instead of 'conceive'?" (Thurtell 2013). There is no opportunity to appreciate our nation's founding and growth by delving much deeper than the text. "Richer" curriculum? I think not.

Over a third of the nation's youth and adult population is overweight or obese. Common Core's "teach to the test" frenzy results in schools cutting class time classes such as PE, art and music. Many schools feel pressured to devote as much time as possible to ELA and mathematics; however, not only is a no-win situation, PE now has ELA standards embedded in its curriculum. That's right. PE is not physical education; it is now ELA in the gym. The Shape of the Nation Report, a study conducted every five years by the National Association for Sport and Physical Education (NASPE) and the American Heart Association (AHA) states: "Physical education classes focus on physical activity—

running, dancing and other movement but physical education also includes health, nutrition, social responsibility, and the value of fitness throughout one's life" (SPARK 2012). PE gives children information and skills to lead healthy lives in many aspects throughout their lives. The downward trend in America's health can be explained, in part, by the downward trend in attitude that PE is not as important as other subjects. In addition, PE, much like recess, is a vital brain-break for students. There is empirical research that clearly demonstrates that physical activity is directly related to students' overall well-being and academic performance (Smart Moves: Why Learning is Not All in your head)

I had to laugh and shake my head when I learned that David Coleman wrote the "Guiding Principles for the Arts, Grades K-12" (Coleman 2012). Coleman even advocates for standardized assessments and data driven instruction here as well, along with integrated ELA standards. Music and art teachers have integrated academics into these subjects for years, and they have done it well. David Coleman has no expertise in art, and apparently did no research into the profound effects art has on a child's development, its implications in therapeutic practices or the benefits of simply having creative outlets. Creativity has been on a downward trend for almost fifteen years, ever since scores SAT's started rising (Rettner 2011). Kyung Hee Kim, a creativity researcher at the College of William and Mary, has studied this phenomenon, and produces solid evidence that since 1990, children have steadily become less able to produce unique or unusual ideas. They are less humorous, less playful, less imaginative and less able to elaborate on ideas, Kim shares. While creativity is innate, it needs to be nurtured, the "use-it-or-lose-it" principle. Along with Kim, Ron Beghetto, an education psychologist at the University of Oregon, attributes the current climate of standardized testing as the primary culprit. Some children only experience art through school. Common Core has hijacked the principles that the people on the ground, the people who know firsthand how to do so without disturbing the value of the artistic experience and creativity, and ruined a good thing. As with PE, schools spend rapidly declining time and resources on these "non-core" pursuits because teaching to the test upsets the balance. Education reform is sucking the life right out of our children.

Why is art such a big deal? Well, first consider the developmental benefits. According to a report by Americans for the Arts, art education, including music, strengthens problem-solving and critical-thinking skills. Art provides experiences in which children use information and make decision through the course of creating art in a variety of forms, using a variety of media and strategies. Art and music is highly creative, and involves math and science, as well, and all of these skills stay with them throughout their lives. "If they are exploring and thinking and experimenting and trying new ideas, then creativity has a chance to blossom," says MaryAnn Kohl, an arts educator and author of numerous books about children's art education (Lynch 2102). Spatial skills are developed through drawing and creating forms through a variety of media such as clay, and children learn skills necessary for interacting with the world that is not composed only of text. Creating art, and talking about it, provides opportunities to learn words for color, action, shapes, and emotions. Art and music are imagination, and imagination leads to problem solving and ideas. Art develops fine motor skills. Students who study music have better geometric reasoning, as well as better attention. "A music-rich experience for children of singing, listening and moving is really bringing a very serious benefit to children as they progress into more formal learning," says Mary Luehrisen, executive director of the National Association of Music Merchants (NAMM) Foundation, a not-for-profit association that promotes the benefits of making music. "There's some good neuroscience research that children involved in music have larger growth of neural activity than people not in music training. When you're a musician and you're playing an instrument, you have to be using more of your brain," says Dr. Eric

Rasmussen, who is the chairman of the Early Childhood Music Department, Peabody Preparatory of The Johns Hopkins University (Brown 2012).

Teaching children to recognize the choices an artist or designer makes in portraying a subject helps kids understand the concept that what they see may be someone's interpretation of reality. Studies show that there is a correlation between art and other achievement. "A report by Americans for the Arts states that young people who participate regularly in the arts (three hours a day on three days each week through one full year) are four times more likely to be recognized for academic achievement, to participate in a math and science fair or to win an award for writing an essay or poem than children who do not participate." Further, "The kind of people society needs to make it move forward are thinking, inventive people who seek new ways and improvements, not people who can only follow directions," says Kohl. "Art is a way to encourage the process and the experience of thinking and making things better!" While Arne Duncan professes to support the arts in schools, "Education in the arts is more important than ever. In the global economy, creativity is essential. Today's workers need more than just skills and knowledge to be productive and innovative participants" (Lynch 2102). Education reform limits the time and resources available to do so. Like physical education, art and music are slowly disappearing from the educational frontier, overshadowed by education reform that professes to want our children to develop these skills, yet ignores long standing evidence on the best ways to do so.

Cursive is yet another skill that has profound effects on the cognitive development of children, but is deemed an antiquated practice by Common Core and is replaced by the need to keyboard. Forming letters by hand helps young children develop fine motor skills and letter recognition, significant in reading and writing (William Klemm 2013). In addition, cursive itself strengthens hand-eye coordination, and engages both hemispheres of the brain, helping with the development of critical brain circuitry. The variations in writing in cursive actually require more mental effort than keyboarding and printing. Key principles of learning and memory are embedded in the process of learning to write, particularly with cursive, and our children are shortchanged by skipping this process.

Common Core's teaching of American history looks different as well. The last decade of education reform has shifted the focus away from teaching American history, and students today are criticized for not know aspects of our history like why America seceded from Britain. They don't know because it is not taught. I want to share an excerpt from Common Core: A Scheme to Rewrite Education "Some Common Core critics have found fault with the 'suggested' textbooks, as well. In history, for example, is A History of US, by Joy Hakim, a comprehensive textbook series on American history almost universally regarded as having a strong liberal bias — and worse. Examination of Hakim's material discloses many errors (including errors of fact, of chronology and of terminology) as well as unjustified assertions and some displays of bias," explained author and historian Alice Whealey in a scathing analysis of the book series for the Textbook League, which reviews educational material for accuracy. She continues: "Joy Hakim should not attempt to write about Western history, particularly the history of Europe, because she obviously hasn't had enough training in these subjects. It is a shame that Oxford University Press has let her get away with so many falsehoods and with such extreme exhibitions of bias." Soon, however, children all across America will be reading the books" (Newman 2013). Remember, too, the earlier discussion about the UN's recommendation that countries "downplay nationality in teaching."

When I started the first grade, my first textbook was a Social Studies book. I was so proud of that book. Finally, I was a real student with a book bag and my own school book. I was a big kid now. I could write my name in and even take it home. I remember opening that book for the first time and seeing a picture of the Golden Gate Bridge. I loved that picture! I remember reading how people came from all over the world to see it, and I remember how uniquely American I thought it was. Are we not uniquely American anymore?

Teaching Values or Indoctrination?

"Schooling is a manufacturing process whereby the raw material called curious boys is turned into products called obedient men."

— **Mokokoma Mokhonoana**

The more I dive into Common Core, the more the movie The Stepford Wives flashes before my eyes, and I shudder at the similarities. Create a robotic population that dresses the same, behaves the same and believes the same—how convenient. And unrealistic.

Merriam-Webster's definition of "indoctrinate" is "to teach (someone) to fully accept the ideas, opinions and beliefs of a particular group and to not consider other ideas, opinions and beliefs" (Encyclopedia Brittanica, Merriam-Webster Unknown). There has been much national discussion about curricula that is aligned with Common Core attempting to indoctrinate students, presenting one set of beliefs as truth, leaving no room for evaluation or consideration of opposing beliefs or evidence. Incorporating leading questions is one method that is cropping up more and more around the country. How does Merriam-Webster define leading question? Like this: "a question so framed as to guide the person questioned in making his reply" (Encyclopedia Brittanica, Merriam-Webster Unknown). Very subtle, but very effective. An example is asking someone what they thought of the horrible play. The question interjects the speaker's opinion with the use of "horrible." It is easy to illicit a response that does not question the word "horrible," even if the answer says something positive about the play. In fact, many people will question their own belief that a play was good just by hearing the question "What did you think of the horrible play?" Humans tend to measure their own opinions by those of others and to avoid being the odd man out. That is why peer pressure is so effective.

Eleventh-graders are taught extensively about the UN's Millennium Development Goals Building Cultural Bridges. Unit 5, Solving the World's Problems, is particularly interesting. Starting on page 382, the UN's Goals are listed as if they are the goals of the US. Students are asked to write about the goals and to consider issues from a global perspective. The material is presented as truth, and is not designed for discussion about global versus what an individual country needs. There is no possibility presented for the goals not being valid in this country, instead, the unit is dedicated to teaching why they are needed (International Baccalaureate 2013). A good clue about the mindset of the curriculum is the fact that the material is located on the World School/International Baccalaureate website. If Bill Gates and his corporate compadres have their way, public schools will produce in mass quantities preprogrammed activists for the issues they deem important. Another fine example of indoctrination. And we provide the tax dollars to pay for it.

A substitute teacher in North Carolina recently sent Glenn Beck a copy of a poem that she claims roughly 80 fifth-grade students recited for their promotion ceremony, at a school near Raleigh. Now, I would expect such a poem to celebrate school being done for the year, and to talk about friendship, memories, and fun. Instead, the poem praises Common Core. The poem is called We Learned More With Common Core, (Ritz 2013) and the phrase is repeated over and over again. It reads:

Text genre, features & theme to explore

We learned more with common core.

Fractions, decimals, journal prompts galore

We learned more with common core.

RUNNER & CUBES are strategies for

Learning more with common core.

Vocab words like (clouds, organs, force), & omnivore

We learned more with common core

Economy, government, Revolutionary war

We learned more with common core.

So many new concepts to explore

We learned more with common core.

I don't know about you, but I find that disturbing and objectionable. If for nothing else, it's simply not true.

As another example, second graders at a number of schools are presented with ELA assignments using the following text:

The job of a president is not easy.
answer: A president's job is not easy.

The people of a nation do not always agree
answer: The nation's people do not always agree.

The choices of a president affect everyone.
answer: The president's choices affect everyone.

He makes sure the laws of the country are fair.
answer: He makes sure the country's laws are fair.

The commands of government officials must be obeyed by all.
answer: The government official's commands must be obeyed by all.

The wants of an individual are less important than the well-being of the nation.

answer: The individual's wants are less important than the well-being of the nation (Schoen 2013).

The "commands" of the government? The Constitution is still alive and well, and it makes it very clear that the government does not "command" anything; rather, it is "allowed" to do certain things, but the power is in the hands of the people.

Fourth grade students in Illinois were given a lesson recently comparing the government and families. You may have heard about this on The Blaze. While the supposed intent was to use analogy to create understanding of the role of government, the lesson instead presented the government in a warm, fuzzy manner as being their family too.

Third graders in several places in the country were given writing homework in which students were asked to read a passage and then respond to the writing prompts. The passage was about a married couple, Ruby and Mike, who apparently are having marital difficulties, compounded by adultery. The story relates how Ruby discovers a bright green hairclip that was not hers nor their daughter's. The questions were designed to draw out emotionally charged responses (Hanson 2013). I was shocked when I ran across this, and it is important to realize that, while I am providing several examples here, there are many, many more of these types of lessons being used in our schools right now.

Did you know that Common Core even has its own search engine? It's called SIRS, and it is specially designed for student research. The SIRS website even proudly displays a banner on the home page "Common Core Approved."

SIRS Knowledge Source (SKS) provides a portal to relevant, credible information carefully hand-selected by our SIRS editorial staff. When students use SKS, they receive best-of content designed to support student research, study, and homework in key curricula subjects. Databases cross-searchable within SKS will vary based on subscription. SIRS Knowledge Source offers

National, State, Province and Common Core Standards aligned to content (ProQuest 2012).

SIRS allows for conducting a search that covers all of its databases, or you may select from one of the following databases for a more targeted search:

SIRS Issues Researcher—Covering the pros and cons of the leading Issues most studied and debated by students

SIRS Government Reporter—Historic and Government Documents, Directories and Almanacs

SIRS Renaissance—Current perspectives on the arts and humanities

SIRS WebSelect—Collection of editorially-selected reliable and credible educational website covering all curriculum topics

Given the focused nature of the curriculum, I am not comfortable with a research tool with content that is "hand selected," particularly not when the federal government and corporate gurus are involved. The search engine has already proven to be slanted, affording nothing to support various view on some topics. Common Core claims that it supports critical thinking skills, championing the abilities of students to research and support their views. How are they able to do that if they are forced to use a research tool whose content is carefully pre-selected? Research should not be conducted using resources that are "Common Core Approved."

You will want to take note as well that the search engine is only available to students at school. Parents cannot access SIRS, which I have a problem with, especially because it violates the Protection of Pupil Rights Act (20 U.S.C. § 1232h; 34 CFR Part 98) which grants parents the right to inspect all instructional material.

(a) Inspection of instructional materials by parents or guardians
All instructional materials, including teacher's manuals, films, tapes, or other supplementary material which will be used in connection with any survey, analysis, or evaluation as part of any applicable program shall be available for inspection by the parents or guardians of the children.

I have found numerous articles written about the experiences of parents who went to the schools and accessed SIRS there. While the creators of SIRS claim to have filtered out material that is inappropriate for students to access, one parent pulled up a chart that highlighted which states allowed for abortions without parental consent. There was also a lesson about Planned Parenthood. In addition, one article recounted that "…when typing in key search words like "traditional marriage" or "heterosexual" or even "pro-life," the site has nothing to offer" (France 2013). Do you see anything wrong with that? I do.

Our Constitution provides the separation of church and state, which basically means the federal government, will not interfere with nor promote any religion. Religion, or no religion, is a personal matter in which the government is not to ever interfere. Public schools are not to incorporate material that helps or hurts any one religion as well. A general discussion about the existence of various religions is appropriate—delving into one, or advocating for it, is not. Neither is attempting to disparage another.

Earlier this year, sixth graders were given an assignment entitled "Is the book of Ruth feminist?" as part of a world literature course. I cannot properly site it because it was an inappropriate lesson that was shared in a closed group on Facebook; however, it really stuck with me and I wanted to bring it up here. I appreciate a good debate as well as various opinions on any topic when it is presented in an appropriate manner in an appropriate setting. This topic cannot be explored without a complete understanding of the entire book and its role in Christianity, as well as an understanding of the time in history these events took place. None of this was part of the lesson. Quite frankly, I do not trust the average individual to teach this material with fidelity to Christianity and what God intended. Not only that, this is theology, not World Literature, and I find its inclusion in a public school curriculum to be inappropriate. If it is part of a Christian school curriculum and is taught with fidelity to the Bible, I think it would be an interesting discussion. What happened to the separation of Church and State?

And then there's the Common Core GED, which now puts its own spin on 9/11. It now portrays the terrorists as "poor Afghanies" (Oleg Atbashian 2013). The author also produces an excerpt from a larger Social Studies Extended Response, found on page 52 from Writing Across the Tests: Responding to Text on the Language Arts, Social Studies, and Science Test, entitled, "Does Foreign Aid Really Help?"

Those who support sending aid to poor countries do so because poor countries often have high levels of poverty, poor educational systems, an ineffective police and judicial force, and limited public services such as healthcare, transportation networks, and banking systems. They believe that when living conditions are this poor, crime levels tend to be higher. Poorer countries, because they have weak governments, often have areas that attract terrorist groups because no one is there to stop them from pursuing those types of activities. Thus, poor countries are often home to terrorist groups that are free to plan and carry out attacks on the rich, industrialized nations, without fear of being stopped. This is in fact [bold words are mine] what happened on 9/11 when terrorists from Afghanistan hijacked planes and carried out attacks on the United States. In this case, the terrorists originated in a country that had received large amounts of foreign aid from rich countries. .

Here is the writing prompt which follows the reading:

Should rich countries continue to give aid to poor countries, or should they stop giving aid? Develop an argument that supports your position, and make sure to use specific details to help develop your ideas.

When students are required to generate ideas, attitudes, and cognitive strategies based on the misleading material that blatantly misrepresents the 9/11 hijackers, who were, for the most part, educated Muslim Arabs from well-to-do families from countries that do provide plenty of foreign aid to support Islamic extremists. Indoctrination and leading questions seem to be the standard of the Common Core Standards.

Oleg Atbashian is a former teacher in Russia, and the Washington Post recently published an article in which he discusses this quite extensively. In it he states: "Having lived and started my working career as a teacher in the USSR, I remember the imposition of identical, centrally planned curriculum on every cookie-cutter school nationwide. The main reason for such mandatory conformity was to maintain a total ideological control and compliance with policies of the totalitarian government. All other aspects of education were secondary to that prime directive…What possible purpose can centralized education have in the United States if not to channel the same ideological conformity to American students, making it easier for the federal bureaucracy to control the educational content?...As history and culture of the Department of Education indicate, this isn't a mere theoretical projection. The educational career and legacy of Bill Ayers alone should raise enough red flags not to allow any centralized educational system to be implemented. Even if it may appear benign at first, the prevailing political tendencies in today's academia will inevitably turn such a system into a conduit of ideological indoctrination. Once Common Core is nationally implemented and federally enforced, public education will become just another word for a forcible indoctrination of our children to induce them to give up their parents' political, social, or religious beliefs and attitudes and to accept contrasting regimented ideas…This is the dictionary definition of brainwashing." I agree.

Global warming is a topic that is strewn all through curricula for most grade levels. The material provides the approach that global temperatures are increasing, followed by two theories that explain it—human industrial activity and population growth. However, the curricula omits the existence of other scientific data and theories, for example, the normal cyclical nature of Earth's climate and the impact of solar activity on Earth's temperatures. Instead, it remains focused on man-made global warming, politicizing the "scientific" presentation of information and promoting the very view that politicians who have a vested interest in tightening government regulations, allowing for greater control over the economy, translating to greater control over people's lives. Typically students are asked to write about how "human activity has directly contributed to the rise in the concentration of greenhouse gases in the Earth's atmosphere," using "multiple pieces of evidence from the text to support their answer." The text is limited to one group's views, presented as truth, and the students are forced to accept it. Indoctrination.

Let's Talk About Sex: National Sexuality Education Standards

"Plans are underway to replace the family, community and church with propaganda, mass-media and education (schooling)...people are only little plastic lumps of dough."
....The perfect organization of the hive with the anthill. Standardized testing would cause the lower classes to confront their biological inferiority, sort of like wearing a dunce cap. In time that would discourage reproduction of the ants on the anthill." - H. H. Cadard, chairman for the Psychology Department at Princeton.

The Planned Parenthood website attempts to explain sex to teenagers. The website provides this definition in its teen section: "People define 'sex' in different ways. The Merriam-Webster dictionary defines it as "sexually motivated behavior." This sounds right to us. But not everyone agrees with the dictionary or with us. People all have their own definitions of what 'sex' and 'having sex' means. For some people it's only penis-in-vagina intercourse. For some people, it's only penis-in-anus intercourse (anal sex). For some people, it's genital rubbing without intercourse. For some people, it includes oral / genital contact. For some, it includes masturbation. The possibilities are many. For most experts (like Merriam-Webster and us), it includes all of the above. However you define it, being sexual with another person — whether that means kissing, touching, or intercourse — involves a lot of responsibility. It's very important to protect yourself against pregnancy and sexually transmitted infections. And you need to make decisions about protection before you engage in vaginal, anal, or oral sex" (Planned Parenthood 2012).

I am, however, looking at Merriam-Webster's definition of sex, and this is what it says:

: the state of being male or female

: men or male animals as a group or women or female animals as a group

: physical activity in which people touch each other's bodies, kiss each other, etc.

: physical activity that is related to and often includes sexual intercourse

Full Definition of SEX

1 : either of the two major forms of individuals that occur in many species and that are distinguished respectively as female or male especially on the basis of their reproductive organs and structures

2 : the sum of the structural, functional, and behavioral characteristics of organisms that are involved in reproduction marked by the union of gametes and that distinguish males and females

3a : sexually motivated phenomena or behavior
b : SEXUAL INTERCOURSE

4 : GENITALIA

Further, it provides a definition for kids:

Etymology: Middle English sex "category of living things according to reproductive roles," from Latin sexus (same meaning)

1 : either of two groups into which many living things are divided according to their roles in reproduction and which consist of males or females

2 : the physical and behavioral characteristics that make males and females different from each other

3 : sexual activity; especially : SEXUAL INTERCOURSE (Encyclopedia Brittanica, Merriam-Webster n.d.)

Notice that the primary definition for children is the difference between males and females.

Education regarding the physiological differences between males and females was called sex education, or sex ed, up until a few years ago. Now it is "sexuality" education. Sexuality has a very different meaning. Here is what Merriam-Webster says about "sexuality":

: the sexual habits and desires of a person

Full Definition of SEXUALITY

: the quality or state of being sexual:

a : the condition of having sex

b : sexual activity

c : expression of sexual receptivity or interest especially when excessive

Here is the one for kids:

Function: noun

: the quality or state of being sexual (Encyclopedia Brittanica, Merriam-Webster)

Do you see the distinct difference? When did we move from sex education in schools, once traditionally providing education regarding gender differences and reproduction, along with basic, common sense health and hygiene considerations, to sexuality education?

I will tell you when. Sexuality became part of the picture when Planned Parenthood managed to work its way into the education arena. Because their influence has been worthy of attention, I am going to share more of what I have learned about Planned Parenthood over the past six months.

Here is a bit more from Planned Parenthood's website:

"What if I don't want to have sex with anyone, ever?

Many people feel this way at various times in their lives. It's perfectly normal. People have different levels of sexual desire — some have more and some have less. Some people would be happy to have sex every day, and some people would be happy to have sex once a month, or less often, or not at all. Many things can affect our desire for sex. They include stress, hormones, how comfortable we are with our partners, past sexual experiences, if we feel safe, how much we're attracted to someone, illness, medication, and many other factors in our lives" (Planned Parenthood 2012).

No mention of "that's a great choice, especially if you are a teenager or not married." No hint that this is in any way a potentially positive decision. How many children under the age of 18 access this website on a daily basis?

Mary Black, veteran educator and "As an educator, I admit the poor standards are not my major concern," she said. "It is what comes along with the standards that is most concerning." Black cited a number of special interest groups as examples, such as Planned Parenthood, explaining that Planned Parenthood and its resources will be given access to American children. Highlighting some of the controversial material — such as asking students to identify different types of "family structures" — she urged parents—and I do too—to read the standards carefully. These standards conflict with beliefs that both liberals and conservatives treasure. The material will often fly in the face of morals and values parents want to instill in their children. The standards, which require that teachers literally belittle the beliefs of what research shows are held by a majority of students, full of intolerance, a backhanded attack against some of the very things Common Core proponents preach against (Newman 2013)

The UN's International Guidelines on Sexuality Education (UNESCO n.d.), on which the National Sexuality Education Standards (Planned Parenthood, The Sex Information and Education Council of the United States n.d.) are based, states that it provides "An evidence informed approach to effective sex, relationships and HIV/STI education." Is it part of Common Core? Yes, it is, although it is a piece that they covered in many shades of gray. A Special Publication of the Journal of School Health (American School Health Association n.d.), states on page 6,"The National Sexuality Education Standards were further informed by the work of the CDC's Health Education Curriculum Analysis Tool (HECAT)3; existing state and international education standards that include sexual health content; the Guidelines for Comprehensive Sexuality Education: Kindergarten – 12th Grade; and the Common Core State Standards for English Language Arts and Mathematics, recently adopted by most states." As I mentioned earlier, they slid it in and are trying to disguise it as a health measure. The publication drops another clue by saying, "Specifically, the National Sexuality Education Standards were developed to address the inconsistent implementation of sexuality education nationwide and the limited time allocated to teaching the topic." The whole idea behind Common Core is to create universal standards for everything. I want to know who would think they know what information was appropriate and at what age my child should learn this "appropriate" information.

Planned Parent, along with The Sex Information and Education Council of the United States (SEICUS), which has now been renamed and is the Sexuality Information and Education Council of the United States, collaborated to develop these standards. Let me introduce two specific board members (Planned

Parenthood, The Sex Information and Education Council of the United States n.d.) who helped author the National Sexuality Education Standards:

Robert McGarry, EdD, is the Director of Training and Curriculum Development of the Gay, Lesbian and Straight Education Network (GLSEN). Let me clarify now that my issue is not with sexual orientation; rather, my issue is that this is in not a discussion that belongs in public schools, and I do not believe that the authors of such standards are qualified to do so. Period. This is a personal discussion to take place at home. The end. Another fine member of the writing team is Cynthia Lam of Sex, Etc. Teen Editorial Staff. Cynthia has been writing for Sex, Etc since she was 14, and she is currently 17. She is still a minor, and she feels she is in a place to make recommendations for discussing sexuality with my child? I don't think so.

The standards take parents' rights to decide what is developmentally appropriate for children. Here are some highlights from the standards themselves:

On page 12 it states:

"By the end of 2nd grade, students should be able to: Use proper names for body parts, including male and female anatomy."

On page 14 it states this:

"By the end of 5th grade, students should be able to: Describe male and female reproductive systems including body parts and their functions. Identify medically-accurate information about female and male reproductive anatomy. Define sexual orientation as the romantic attraction of an individual to someone of the same gender or a different gender."

And on page 9 under "Guiding Values and Principles" it gives us this:

"Instruction by qualified sexuality education teachers is essential for student achievement." Achievement at what? Who decides who is "qualified"? Because I will state out loud right now, there is nobody affiliated with Planned Parenthood who is qualified in my eyes. And that's my choice, just as it is yours.

The National Sexuality Education Standards proceed to state:

"Students need opportunities to engage in cooperative and active learning strategies, and sufficient time must be allocated for students to practice skills relating to sexuality education." Exactly what does that mean? What specific activities are they "cooperating" on, and what skills are they "actively" learning, and just what are the students supposed to be "practicing"? I can't even wrap my mind around this one!

And then there is this little gem:

"Students need multiple opportunities and a variety of assessment strategies to determine their achievement of the sexuality education standards and performance." Performance?

The National Sexuality Education Standards have already reared its ugly head in a number of classrooms across the country in the form of a book called It's Perfectly Normal: Changing Bodies, Growing Up, Sex, and Sexual Health. "It's Perfectly Normal" has been used in the lower elementary grades, and addresses sex, sexuality, masturbation, contraception, homosexuality, oral sex, and abortion. A prison in Washington rejected it because it is so graphic, calling it pornographic (Skalicky, Common Core: "Sexuality" Education 2013). Apparently it's ok for our young children, though.

The book contains graphic illustrations of adult nude men and women, and encourages children to explore their own sexuality. It demonstrates how to masturbate, and describes sexual intercourse by saying it "can involve the penis and vagina, or the mouth and the genitals, or the penis and the anus." Let me stop right here and say that this is not a commentary on the rightness or wrongness of homosexuality. It is a commentary on inappropriate lessons in our schools, conversations that need take place at home with parents, not in the schools.

The book never discusses chastity or abstinence. Further, it disparages some religious beliefs by stating "And some religions call masturbation a sin. But masturbating cannot hurt you." Many believe that sexual activity should not take place outside of marriage, yet this is never presented as an option. Children are simply encouraged to explore sexual activity as normal, but not sacred or intimate.

Planned Parenthood: Current Report that shows that when Planned Parenthood is NOT present, teenage pregnancy goes down. "(Washington, DC) Contrary to the Planned Parenthood Federation of America public relations and lobbying message, there is no correlation with PPFA community presence and reduced teen pregnancy. In contrast, teen pregnancies actually decreased with the absence of PPFA. So concludes a major meta-study released by American Life League, the nation's oldest pro-life Catholic education and advocacy group. "We know that the pro-abortion first-response will be 'Consider the source.' But American Life League is not the source; the source is the official records of 16 counties within the Texas panhandle," said Rita Diller, national director of ALL's STOPP International project. "From 1994 through 2010, Planned Parenthood facilities in these counties went from 19 to zero. In the same period, the teen pregnancy rate dropped almost in half, from 43.6 per 1,000 to 24.1 per thousand, and the population of teen girls aged 13-17 remained stable. Those aren't our numbers; those are government numbers." "People don't realize that Planned Parenthood must work hard to replace the 43 percent of its customers it loses each year," added Diller. "It normally does this by promoting sexual promiscuity to teens. This study suggests that, when Planned Parenthood leaves, teens are more likely to embrace chastity" (Hart n.d.).

A new meta-study, conducted by ALL's Stop Planned Parenthood International (STOPP) Project, found that "Three primary rationales used for taxpayer funding of Planned Parenthood----women's wellness, reduction of teen pregnancy, and serving the poor----are invalid." It further states in its report that "Planned Parenthood publically maintains that its role in reproductive health serves the American public at large by educating teens on "safe sex," providing contraceptives, and reducing pregnancies. Critics claim that PPFA's view that even kindergartners are sexual beings results in just the opposite: Sex education that encourages more sex in general and the onset of participation in sexual intercourse at earlier ages. In its fact sheet Reducing Teen Pregnancy, 6 PPFA proposes to reduce the quantity of teen pregnancies through a number of initiatives" (Brendan Clowes 2013) Not one of the initiatives includes incorporating one of the several proven programs for teaching abstinence.

Planned Parenthood has a very liberal approach to sex education, note the switch to the word "sexuality", and from everything I researched, they promote promiscuity. A friend of mine shared with me that she once ran four abortion clinics in Texas. The standard practice was to give the teenagers who came into the clinic very low dosages of birth control pills so that if they weren't exactly 24 hours apart in taking them, the risk of pregnancy was high. It was a business decision.

Education expert Dr. Duke Pesta created a video for The New American about the nationwide school standards for history, science, and sexuality (Newman, Education Expert: Common Core Education is Social Engineering 2013). Dr. Pesta, academic director at Freedom Project Education and an English professor at the University of Wisconsin, is clear that the overarching goals is social engineering and simply denying truth, and this is an argument that numerous other prominent experts and educators across the nation also make. "Many states across the union are having second thoughts," said Pesta. ""We have word of a pending danger," he explained "We now have a sense of what the health standards are going to look like, what the science standards are going to look like, and what the history standards are going to look like. They are as bad, or worse, than what we already have." He cited national "health" standards, "which advertise teaching our kids health and sexuality skills from kindergarten to 12th grade…I don't know about you, but the idea that we're going to send our kids to public schools to learn sexuality skills is very disturbing… One of the numerous complaints is that children will be required to 'identify different kinds of family structures," meaning, homosexual and transgender, and students will be expected to "provide arguments as to why all different types of families are equal."

Pesta further notes that the consequences "are grave," noting that only a limited view would be taught. "No longer do moms and dads get to educate their kids at home about their views on sexuality," he said. "The state standards mandate that every kid in kindergarten, first, and second grade engage in these exercises." "By the time kids reach third grade, he continued, "they will have to make arguments explaining why there is no such thing as gender biology."

Dr. Pesta strongly notes that the real agenda behind the federalization of education is clear. "It is an education that fundamentally denies truth, not just in the humanities and history, but alarmingly, as we've seen, in science, math, and biology," he said. "It's all done for social engineering aims," he added. "This is what's coming. Common Core is bad now — it's going to get a lot, lot worse."

Special Education/504 Plan Students

"Everybody is a genius. But if you judge a fish by it's ability to climb a tree, it will live its whole life believing that it is stupid." --Albert Einstein

Here is what the Common Core website says about students with disabilities and those learning the English language:

FAQ: What does this work mean for students with disabilities and English language learners? The Common Core State Standards give states the opportunity to share experiences and best practices, which can lead to an improved ability to serve young people with disabilities and English language learners. Additionally, the standards include information on application of the standards for these groups of students (Achieve, Common Core State Standards Initiative 2012).

Special needs students will still have individual educational programs (IEP's), but how they will integrated individual needs and abilities based on the Common Core Standards is causing grave concern. Remember that ALL students are require to meet the same standards. As a matter of fact, Common Core requires that curricula not be modified any longer to accommodate special education students, which violates the Individuals with Disabilities Education Act (IDEA) and many of the access provisions of the Americans with Disabilities Act (ADA), sending us about 50 years back in time. Students can have supports in place, but a modified curriculum is often necessary for some students to benefit from instruction (Steinhagen 2013).

IEP's are to provide specialized, individualized instruction tailored to meet a student's needs so the he or she can benefit as much as possible from education. IEP's include alternative assessments when best for the student, as well as supports and services necessary for a child to benefit from an education. Common Core creates a standard education and standardized assessment. Standard and individualized contradict each other. It's either one or the other, not both.

Many children who have IEP's need minimal supports in school. Many more have significant disabilities or other special needs that realistically will prevent them from meeting any set of standards. IEP's are developed based on where they are right now and what reasonable expectations are for growth. A tenth grader may be reading at a seventh grade level and successful in math at a fifth grade level, but his educational needs are no less important than the gifted child working on college preparatory courses. His abilities and needs are different and should be met, without demoralizing him with a sudden shift in expectations brought on by Common Core and standardized tests. It sounds wonderful to align IEP's with Common Core, and there are several books and websites that cheerfully claim help teachers do just that. The truth is, it doesn't work. Forcing all special education students to master standards that many simply cannot do is cruel.

This is from the CC standards themselves... Access for Students with Disabilities (MATH):

The Common Core Standards articulate rigorous expectations in the areas of mathematics, reading, writing, and speaking and listening in order to prepare students to be college- and career-ready. These standards identify the knowledge and skills students must acquire in order to be successful. Research shows that students with disabilities are capable of high levels of learning and should not be limited by low expectations and watered down curriculum. It is imperative that these highly capable students—

regardless of their disability—are held to the same expectations articulated in the Core Standards as other students.

However, how these high standards are taught is of the utmost importance in reaching students with special needs.

When learning the knowledge and skills represented in the Core Standards, students with disabilities may need accommodations or in exceptional cases modified goals, incorporated in an individualized education program (IEP), to help them access information or demonstrate their knowledge. Students might be precluded from reaching particular standards given the nature of the standard itself. In instances when a standard asks students to perform actions they are physically incapable of, students will need to be presented with alternative options to demonstrate similar knowledge and skills within the range of their abilities. Accommodations based on individual needs allow students of all disability levels to learn within the framework of the Core (Achieve, Common Core State Standards Initiative 2012).

Standardized testing will be different as well. The test moderator may read the directions to the students, but may no longer read the test itself. That fails many students with learning disabilities right off the bat. It's like telling a carpet to stay suspended in mid-air and then pulling out all of the tables and "supports" from under. It not possible, and it is not fair to these students. Children who struggle for accomplishment, who search for meaning in this world, will have the wind knocked out of them. A child who reads two or three grade levels below his counterparts of the same age is not going to suddenly be cured in one year. IEP's will be written to the standards, and children will not be able to meet the goals. What are the chances of doing well on the assessments? This forces schools to push special education students out the door, and this has already happened. The alternative is to punish the teacher because test scores are poor, erroneously interpreted as a result of ineffective instruction. I believe that this is intentional, and that one of the goals is to weed out special education students, who will ultimately be placed in special schools, as they were decades ago, and that this is being set up by the standards and the attempt to shift the education system away from the current public school system and to a charter school system.

The National Center for Learning Disabilities (NCLB) is clearly pro-Common Core, but even they had to admit the glaring risks of standardized testing for students with disabilities:

Increased grade retention: Large performance gaps exist between students with disabilities (including LD) and their non-disabled peers. Students with disabilities continue to be retained, or held back, much more often than the general education students. Promotion tests – the fastest growing area of high-stakes testing – will most likely contribute to even more grade retention of students with LD, despite the fact that retention has been shown to be an ineffective way of improving academic achievemen

Awarding of alternative high school diplomas or certificates: Many states are developing one or more alternative diplomas and certificates for students with disabilities who fail high school graduation tests. These include nonstandard diplomas such as IEP diplomas, certificates of completion, certificates of attendance, and modified diplomas. There is little research on the value of such alternative diplomas and certificates, but it is likely that many will not be accepted by colleges and universities.

Awarding of alternative high school diplomas or certificates: Many states are developing one or more alternative diplomas and certificates for students with disabilities who fail high school graduation tests. These include nonstandard diplomas such as IEP diplomas, certificates of completion, certificates of attendance, and modified diplomas. There is little research on the value of such alternative diplomas and certificates, but it is likely that many will not be accepted by colleges and universities (Cortellia 2013).

Essentially, risks that already exist for students with disabilities will be compounded by Common Core.

Common Core boasts that it makes a high quality education available to all students, including those with disabilities. Common Core falsely claims that expectations have traditionally been lowered for students with disabilities, depriving them of a full education. Common Core pretends to ride in on a white horse and rescue students with disabilities. I have been involved with special education for years, personally and professionally, and I am dismayed that Common Core dishonestly claims to be good for special education students. Special education teachers and parents all over the country spend countless hours devising unique learning strategies, plans and goals based on individual children's current capabilities and needs. While many students may not advance to the level of their same-aged peers, they advance as much as is possible, opening up possibilities that were not present even twenty years ago. Common Core pulls the rug out from under individualized planning, and all of the supports in the world are not going to magically enable students to meet goals that they are not physiologically able to meet. Students with disabilities already struggle with not feeling good enough, and Common Core will throw that message needlessly right in their faces.

When I was in school, I had undiagnosed ADD, and was also gifted. I did not test well. My scores were mediocre on the ACT and PSAT, yet anyone who spent any time with me knew I was above average in intelligence and capabilities. The private college I attended normally required high scores on one or the other; they made the exception for me because the test scores did not accurately represent the student and they have plenty of other data to base that decision upon. If Common Core had existed back then, I can assure you that I would have been the student held back because of a test score, and I would gotten frustrated and dropped out. Imagine how drastically different my life would have been. Now think about that in the context of today's students. Lives will be forever changed because of Common Core, and that's not a good thing.

Over the years, we have been able to offer special needs students the opportunities to learn according to their needs and according to their unique learning styles. The glimmer of hope these children hold so dearly will be extinguished by the stormy winds of Common Core.

Final Thoughts

Blood has been shed for your freedom to speak on political and social issues, don't waste it by being silent when our country is gasping for breath.

– Caroline Harris

I never thought I would write a book that I hoped disturbed its readers, but I have, and this is it. I hope reading what I have written has alarmed you enough that each of you will start questioning, researching, talking and acting.

A few weeks ago, Arne Duncan rudely commented that the biggest opponents of Common Core are "suburban white moms who suddenly realized their kids aren't as brilliant as they thought they were." While I had the urge initially to kick him in the teeth, I realized that the only reason he has become nastier than usual is because the efforts that parents have put forth thus far, are working. If they weren't, he would just ignore us. People who are presenting something honorable don't fight ugly, don't have to lie to sell it, don't have to sneak in bits and pieces of it, calling it something else, and don't have to force people to accept. If it's good, people will want it.

It was simply impossible to present everything I wanted to in one book. The Common Core issue runs much, much deeper. Perhaps there is another book in the works. Regardless, I urge you to read, to keep up with current events regarding Common Core, to start talking with other parents, to participate in a few groups on social media, and to act. There are changes coming about almost every day—new information and new activity—on the Common Core frontier, and it is important to stay informed. We got sleepy and Common Core snuck in. This cannot happen again. I recognize we are all short on spare time; however, a letter to a congressman, opting out of, or refusing, standardized testing, and learning, learning, learning…are powerful and meaningful actions to take.

As I progress in my journey through the heart of Common Core, sifting through the lies and smoke screens to uncover the truth, I am appalled that our country's leadership has not only allowed this to happen, it perpetuated it. Current events will not go unchecked, however. The parents of this country—moms, dads, grandparents and guardians alike—have made their voices heard already, and will continue to do so. Several states are dropping Common Core, others are peeling it back one layer at a time, parents are opting out of the test, home schooling has risen dramatically because of Common Core, and even InBloom and Bill Gates were recently asked to leave Colorado. Arne Duncan has attempted to smokescreen the real issues by playing the race card and the "mom" card, trying to divide us to distract us, which are all big mistakes. America is smarter than that. Common Core is not about race, gender, religion, political affiliation or economic status of the country's citizens. It is about children, and what is best for them. We cannot lose sight of that, ever. We will not be divided, we will not waiver, and we will not be silent. We will do what is right, even when it's hard.

"First they ignore you, then they laugh at you, then they fight you, when you win." –**Ghandi**

Bibliography

101, Treason. 2008. Exposing Government/Corporate Corruption. March 15. Accessed October 16, 2013. http://treason123.blogspot.com/2008/03/lots-of-infoget-educated-great-sites-to.html.

2009. A Global Fund for Education: Achieving Education for All. August Unknown. Accessed September 14, 2013. http://www.brookings.edu/research/papers/2009/08/education-gartner.

Achieve. 2002. Achieve. January 2. Accessed September 14, 2013. http://www.achieve.org/.

—. 2012. Common Core State Standards Initiative. January 1. Accessed November 18, 2013. http://www.corestandards.org/.

—. 2012. "Public License." Common Core State Standards Initiative. January 1. Accessed November 18, 2013. http://www.corestandards.org/public-license.

—. 2013. "Understanding the Skills of the Common Core Education Standards." CTE: Learning That Works for America. January 1. Accessed September 29, 2013. http://www.careertech.org/career-clusters/ccresources/commoncoreresource.html.

Achieve, Inc. 2008. Benchmarking for Success: Ensuring U.S. Students Receive a World-class Education. December 18. Accessed October 7 2013. http://www.achieve.org/BenchmarkingforSuccess.

Alexander, Rachel. 2013. Common Core for All. September 30. Accessed October 9, 2013. http://townhall.com/columnists/rachelalexander/2013/09/30/common-core-for-all-n1712871/page/full.

American School Health Association. n.d. National Sexuality Education Standards: Core Content and Skills, K-12. A Special Publication of the Journal of School Health. Special Report. http://eric.ed.gov/?id=ED528427.

Apollo. 2012. "The Rockefeller School System: Compulsory Indoctrination Camps for Social Control." The Arrows of Truth. November 1. Accessed September 7, 2013http://thearrowsoftruth.com/the-rockefeller-school-system-compulsory-indoctrination-camps-for-social-control/. http://thearrowsoftruth.com/the-rockefeller-school-system-compulsory-indoctrination-camps-for-social-control/.

Author, Sandra Stotsky and Jane. 2013. Common Core Is State-Led? Hardly! June 28. Accessed September 5, 2013. http://americanprinciplesproject.org/preserve-innocence/2013/common-core-is-state-led-hardly/.

Bean, Angela. 2013. "Parents – Don't be deceived about data collecting on your children." The Citizen. August 13. http://www.thecitizen.com/articles/08-13-2013/parents-%E2%80%93-don%E2%80%99t-be-deceived-about-data-collecting-your-children.

Beck, Glenn. 2013. "Did Bill Gates Admit the Real Purpose of Common Core?" Glenn Beck. Dallas, Texas, September 13. http://www.glennbeck.com/2013/09/24/did-bill-gates-admit-the-real-purpose-of-common-core/.

2013. "BILL GATES SPENDING MILLIONS ON COMMON CORE DEVELOPMENT AND PROMOTION." Citizes United for Responsible Education. Unknown Unknown. Accessed September 26, 2013. http://www.natcure.org/who-is-controlling-education/bill-gates-unesco/.

Brendan Clowes, Rita Diller, Robert Gasper, Paul Rondeau, Jim Sedlak. 2013. "Planned Parenthood

Federation ofAmerica: A 5-Part Analysis of Business Practices, Community Outcomes,and Taxpayer Funding." STOPP-American Life League. http://www.stopp.org/PPFAReports/PPFA_2013_Report.pdf.

Brown, Laura Lewis. 2012. The Benefits of Music Education. Unknown Unknown. Accessed October 29, 2013. http://www.pbs.org/parents/education/music-arts/the-importance-of-art-in-child-development/.

Bush, George W. 2002. President Signs Landmark No Child Left Behind Bill. Hamilton, Ohio, January 08. http://georgewbush-whitehouse.archives.gov/news/releases/2002/01/20020108-1.html.

Carey, Colette. 2011. While our students nationwide take mandatory tests – who is evaluating the evaluators? September 15. Accessed October 29, 2013. http://www.axs.tv/press_articles/dan-rather-reports-studies-standardized-test-scores/.

Carol Burris, Kevin Welner. 2013. "An Open Letter of Concern Regarding New York State's APPR Legislation ." NewYorkPrincipals.org. October 3. Accessed October 15, 2013. http://nepc.colorado.edu/publication/letter-to-Arne-Duncan.

Caroline Porter, Stephanie Banchero. 2013. More US Schools Go International. June 16. Accessed October 17, 2013. http://online.wsj.com/news/articles/SB10001424127887324049504578545852284235028.

Center for Media and Democracy. 2012. ALEC Exposed. July 10. Accessed October 22, 2013. http://www.alecexposed.org/wiki/ALEC_Exposed.

Christel Swasey, Emmett McGroarty, Sherena Arrington, David Cox, interview by Glenn Beck. 2013. Harming Education (Common Core Abuses Children) (March 14).

Citizen, NC. 2013. Dr. James Milgram Opposes the Common Core State Standards-Why? July 14. Accessed October 9, 2013. http://stopcommoncorenc.org/2013/07/14/dr-james-milgram-opposes-common-core-math-standards-why/.

Clark, Danette. 2013. Pearson Education's creepy vision confirms Common Core fears. http://eagnews.org/pearson-educations-creepy-vision-confirms-common-core-fears/.

Coleman, David. 2012. "Guiding Principles for the Arts, Grades K-12." NYSED.gov. Accessed October 31, 2013. http://usny.nysed.gov/rttt/docs/guidingprinciples-arts.pdf.

2013. "COMMON CORE MOVEMENT IS A TROJAN HORSE AND TIED TO THE UNITED NATIONS." Arizonans Against Common Core. Unknown Unknown. Accessed October 5, 2013. http://arizonansagainstcommoncore.com/UN_connection.html.

Cook, Joshua. 2013. Student Records Hacked Easily: Security Breach Triggers Common Core Rebellion Among Teachers and Parents. November 18. http://freedomoutpost.com/2013/11/student-records-hacked-easily-security-breach-triggers-common-core-rebellion-teachers-parents/.

Cortellia, Candace. 2013. "Parent Advocacy Brief." National Center for Learning Disabilities. Promotion tests.

County, Citizen of Bradley. 2013. Common Core "State-Led"? Think Again. October 4. Accessed October 5, 2013. http://bradleycountynews.wordpress.com/2013/10/04/common-core-state-led-think-again/.

Data Quality Campaign. 2013. "Talking about the Facts of Education Data with Policymakers." Data Quality Campaign. http://www.thecitizen.com/articles/08-13-2013/parents-%E2%80%93-don%E2%80%99t-be-deceived-about-data-collecting-your-children.

David T. Conley, Ph.D. June. "What Does It Take to Be College and Career Ready?" Education Week. 12 2013. Accessed September 19, 2013. http://www.epiconline.org/publications/what-does-it-take-for-students-to-be-ready-for-college-and-career.

2005. "Dewey's Political Philosophy." Stanford University-Stanford Encyclopedia of Philosophy. February 9. Accessed October 1, 2013. http://plato.stanford.edu/entries/dewey-political/.

Dictionary, Merriam-Webster Online. Rigor. Springfield, MA. http://www.merriam-webster.com/.

Dodrill, Tara. 2013. Group Fears Common Core Will Result In National Student Database. September 27. http://www.offthegridnews.com/2013/09/27/group-fears-common-core-will-result-in-national-student-database/.

Downey, Maureen. 2013. Common Core Brand Name: Who Is Making Money Off the New Standards? August 25. Accessed September 13, 2013. http://www.ajc.com/weblogs/get-schooled/2013/aug/25/common-core-brand-name-who-making-money-new-standa/.

Dr. James Milgram, Emmett McGroarty. 2013. Common Core Issues. July 23. Accessed September 29, 2013. http://www.hslda.org/commoncore/topic4.aspx.

Duncan, Arne. 2013. ""The Vision of Education Reform in the United States"." United States Mission to UNESCO.

Paris, October 11. http://unesco.usmission.gov/duncan-remarks.html.

Unknown. "Education for All-History." UNESCO. Unknown Unknown. Accessed September 7, 2013. http://www.unesco.org/new/en/education/themes/leading-the-international-agenda/education-for-all/the-efa-movement.

Education, Career Technical. 2013. CTE: Learning That Works for America. January 1. Accessed September 29, 2013. http://www.careertech.org/career-clusters/ccresources/.

Emmett McGroarty, Jane Robbins. 2013. Common Core Sparks War of Words Among Literature Teachers. January 15. http://www.theblaze.com/contributions/common-core-sparks-war-over-words-among-literature-teachers/ .

Empson, Rip. 2013. News Brief. February 5. Accessed September 16, 2013. http://www.ccsso.org/News_and_Events/Current_News/Wi th_100M_From_The_Gates_Foundation_and_Others_inBl oom_Wants_to_Transform_Education_by_Unleashing_Its_ Data.html.

Encyclopedia Brittanica, Merriam-Webster. Unknown. indoctrinate. Accessed September 1, 2013. http://www.merriam-webster.com/dictionary/indoctrinate.

—. Unknown. leading question. Accessed September 2, 2013. http://www.merriam-webster.com/dictionary/leading%20question.

—. n.d. sex. http://www.merriam-webster.com/dictionary/sex.

—. n.d. sexuality. http://www.merriam-webster.com/dictionary/sexuality?show=0&t=1385254424.

Encylopedia Brittanica, Merriam-Webster. Unknown. assess. Unknown Unknown. Accessed August 29, 2013. http://www.merriam-webster.com/dictionary/assess.

Evaluation and Training Administration. 2011. "Five-Year Research and Evaluation Plan for 2012-2017." United States Department of Labor: Employment and Training Administration. http://wdr.doleta.gov/research/FullText_Documents/ETAO P_2013_21.pdf.

Farley, Todd. 2011. Standardized Testing: A Decade in Review. April 4. Accessed October 15, 2013. http://www.huffingtonpost.com/todd-farley/standardized-testing-a-de_b_846044.html.

2013. "Financing for Global Education." Brookings Institute. September 1. Accessed October 30, 2013. http://www.brookings.edu/~/media/research/files/reports/20 13/09/financing%20global%20education/basic%20educatio n%20financing%20final%20%20webv2.pdf.

Fleisher, Lisa. 2012. Text Book Sales Likely to Rise on New Rules. May 29. Accessed October 29, 2013. http://online.wsj.com/news/articles/SB10001424052702303 67400457743430304060586.

France, Macey. 2013. Common Core-Approved Search Engine. September 25. http://politichicks.tv/column/common-core-approved-search-engines/.

Gates, Bill. 2013. "Annual Letter." Bill and Melinda Gates Foundation. January unknown. Accessed September 19, 2013. http://annualletter.gatesfoundation.org/pdf/2013_AL_Engli sh.pdf.

Given, Casey. 2013. It's Official: The Feds Control Common Core. April 3. Accessed September 4, 2013. http://americansforprosperity.org/legislativealerts/its-official-the-feds-control-common-core/.

Global Partnership for Education, Media Center. 2013. "GLOBAL PARTNERSHIP FOR EDUCATION GRANTS US$439 MILLION FOR QUALITY EDUCATION FOR CHILDREN IN 12 LOW-INCOME COUNTRIES." Global Partnership for Education. May 22. Accessed October 9, 2013. http://www.globalpartnership.org/news/429/762/Global-Partnership-for-Education-Grants-US-439-Million-for-Quality-Education-for-Children-in-12-Low-Income-Countries/.

Govtrack.us. 2013. Bills and Resolutions. November 21. Accessed November 1, 2013. https://www.govtrack.us/congress/bills/.

Greene, Jay P. 2013. Fordham and CC-Backers Need to Get Their Stories Straight. October 31. Accessed November 2, 2013. Fordham and CC-Backers Need to Get Their Stories Straight.

Hanson, Rosalie. 2013. Common Core Reaches a New Low. October 6. http://www.independentsentinel.com/common-core-reaches-a-new-low-check-this-out/.

Hardt, Shane Vander. 2013. Debunking Misconceptions:" The Common Core Was State Led". January 24. Accessed September 2, 2013. http://truthinamericaneducation.com/common-core-state-standards/debunking-misconceptions-the-common-core-is-state-led/.

—. 2013. Lead Writer Jason Zimba Admits Common Core Math Standards Weakness. Washington DC: American

Principles Project. http://fightcommoncore.com/lead-writer-jason-zimba-admits-common-core-math-standards-weakness/.

Hart, Shane Vander. n.d. Major Study Concludes Planned Parenthood Services Don't Reduce Teen Pregnancy. http://caffeinatedthoughts.com/2013/09/major-study-concludes-planned-parenthood-services-dont-reduce-teen-pregnancy/.

Hoge, Anita. 2013. Obama's Dream Come True: Nationalizing Education. October 19. Accessed October 19, 2013. http://www.newswithviews.com/Hoge/anita101.htm.

Home School Legal Defense Association. 2013. Does It Matter That Testing Is Being Aligned with the Common Core? October 15. Accessed November 19, 2013. http://www.hslda.org/docs/nche/000010/200210230.asp.

Horn, Jim. 2012. David Coleman's Global Revenge and the Common Core. April 29. Accessed August 13, 2013. http://www.schoolsmatter.info/2012/04/david-colemans-global-revenge-and.html.

2013. "House Subcommittee Maintains Funding for Basic Education." Basic Education Coalition. July 19. Accessed November 2, 2013. http://www.basiced.org/tag/foreign-aid/.

HSDLA. 2013. "Common Core Issues: Does Common Core Have a Philosophical Bias?" Home School Defense League Association. July 23. Accessed November 1, 2013. http://www.hslda.org/commoncore/topic4.aspx.

Huffington Post. 2013. "Bill Gates: Education Is The One Issue That's Key To America's Future." Huffington Post. January 30. Accessed October 17, 2013. http://www.huffingtonpost.com/2013/01/30/bill-gates-on-education-t_n_2584107.html.

InBloom. 2012. "InBloom Data Store Logica Model-Developer Documentation." InBloom. https://www.inbloom.org/sites/default/files/docs-developer-1.0.68-20130118/ch-data_model-enums.html#type-SexType&#8221.

International Baccalaureate. 2013. "Building Cultural Bridges Unit 5." World School, International Baccalaureate. August. Accessed October 23, 2013. http://www.mvsd-ib.org/ib/wp-content/uploads/2013/08/cb_sb_ela_miu_L5_U5_full_unit_SE_v2.pdf.

International Baccalaureate Organization. 2011. Expanding Student Access to a Rigorous International Education: An IB position paper on the Common Core State Standards CCSS. Unknown Unknown. Accessed September 22, 2013. http://www.ibo.org/iba/commoncore/documents/IBCommonCorePositionStatement.pdf.

Iserbyt, Charlotte. 2000 Ravenna. The Deliberate Dumbing Down of America. Ohio: Conscience Press.

James Millgram, Emmett McGroarty. 2013. Common Core Issues. July 23. Accessed October 1, 2013. http://www.hslda.org/commoncore/topic4.aspx.

Julian, Liam. 2013. "Common Core's Uncommon Rise." Philanthropy Roundtable. Spring Unknown. Accessed November 9, 2013. http://www.philanthropyroundtable.org/topic/excellence_in_philanthropy/common_cores_uncommon_rise.

Kaplan, Sheila. 2013. FERPA, Common Core State Standards, and Data Sharing. http://educationnewyork.com/files/FERPA-ccsss.pdf.

Karen Budd, Elizabeth Carson, Barry Garelick, David Klein, R. James Milgram, Ralph A. Raimi, Martha

Schwartz, Sandra Stotsky, Vern Williams, and W. Stephen Wilson, New York City HOLD and Mathematically Correct. 2005. Ten Myths About Math Education and Why You Should Not Believe Them. May 4. Accessed October 23, 2013. http://www.nychold.com/myths-050504.html.

Kendall, John. 2011. Understanding Common Core Standards. Denver, CO: McRel.

Kibler, Jeffry. 2013. Common Core Based on UN Education Program and Agenda 21. June 3. Accessed August 5, 2013. http://www.thebrennerbrief.com/2013/06/03/common-core-based-on-un-education-program-and-agenda-21/.

Kohn, Alfie. 2000. The Case Against Standardized Testing: Raising the Scores, Ruining the Schools. Portsmouth: Heinemann.

Koler, Duncan. 2012. Research Shows True Agenda of IB Program. November 16. Accessed August 28, 2013. http://www.cdapress.com/columns/my_turn/article_da7f4ea1-626e-5e6f-9071-986e0640e3c7.html.

Labor, United States Department of. 2012. "Funding Opportunity Announcement." DOLETA. http://www.doleta.gov/grants/pdf/wdqi_sga_dfa_py_11_01.pdf.

Landis, Joan, interview by Christel Swasey. 2013. Interview With A Clinical Mental Health Therapist (May 16). http://www.youtube.com/watch?v=DdPz7Eg18jU&feature=share.

Layton, Lyndsey. 2013. Walton foundation pumps $20 million into Teach for America. July 31. Accessed September 14, 2013. http://articles.washingtonpost.com/2013-07-

31/local/40912849_1_teach-for-america-tfa-recruits-dave-levin.

Lee, Matthew Russell. 2012. At UN, Gates Foundation Learns How to Buy Impunity Like Orr's Position. July 2. Accessed September 13, 2013. http://www.innercitypress.com/xb1gatesorr070212.html.

Logue, Gretchen. 2013. "Database in #CommonCore Explained. Segregation Revisited? ." Conservative Teachers of America. March. http://conservativeteachersofamerica.com/tag/gsv-advisors/#sthash.7igN8wPi.dpbs.

Luksik, Peg. 2013. The Federal Hand Behind Common Core. November 5. Accessed November 6, 2013. http://www.crisismagazine.com/2013/the-federal-hand-behind-common-core.

Lynch, Grace Hwang. 2102. The Importance of Art in Child Development. Accessed November 3, 2013. http://www.pbs.org/parents/education/music-arts/the-importance-of-art-in-child-development/.

Malleson, Tom. 2013. "After Occupy: Economic Democracy for the 21st Century." Social Science Computing Operative University of Wisconsin, Madison. Unknown Unknown. Accessed November 7, 2013. http://www.ssc.wisc.edu/~wright/929-utopias-2013/Real%20Utopia%20Readings/Malleson%20-%20Economic%20Democracy%20Book%20.pdf.

Marybeth Sullivan, Legislative Analyst II. 2013. "OLR Research Report." Connecticut General Assemby. October 15. Accessed November 1, 2013. http://www.cga.ct.gov/2013/rpt/2013-R-0344.htm.

Mayer, D. 2012. The ALEC-Stand for Children-Teach for America Connection. May 7. Accessed October 21, 2013.

http://www.greatschoolsforamerica.org/gsa-wp/the-alec-teach-for-america-connection/.

McCauley, Lauren. 2013. As WalMart Writes Checks, Critics Blast Teach for America. August 5. Accessed November 2, 2013. https://www.commondreams.org/headline/2013/08/05-6.

McGowan, Sarah. 2013. Truth Report: The Stress Test-How Today's Standardized Tests Impact Health, Performance and School Culture. April 24. Accessed October 4, 2013. http://www.teentruth.net/voices-insight/truth-report-the-stress-test/.

NAEYC. 2009. Position Statements. Unknown Unknown. Accessed October 27, 2013. http://oldweb.naeyc.org/about/positions/dap3.asp.

—. 2001. STILL Unacceptable Trends in Kindergarten Entry and Placement. Unknown Unknown. Accessed October 27, 2013. http://www.naeyc.org/files/naeyc/file/positions/Psunacc.pdf .

Newman, Alex. 2013. Common Core: A Scheme to Rewrite Education. August 8. Accessed October 11, 2013. http://www.thenewamerican.com/culture/education/item/16 192-common-core-a-scheme-to-rewrite-education.

—. 2013. Education Expert: Common Core Education is Social Engineering. October 18. http://www.thenewamerican.com/culture/education/item/16 762-education-expert-common-core-education-is-social-engineering.

Nichols, John. 2011. ALEC Exposed. August 18. Accessed August 29, 2013. http://www.thenation.com/article/161978/alec-exposed#.

Nielsen, Kris. 2013. Children of the Core. New York: Kris Nielsen.

2013. "No Money, No Vote: A Closer Look at the Strained Relationship Between the U.S. and UNESCO." Cultural Heritage Lawyer. November 13. Accessed November 20, 2013. http://culturalheritagelawyer.blogspot.com/2013/11/no-money-no-vote-closer-look-at.html.

Novak, George. 1960. "John Dewey's Theories of Education." International Socialist Review. Edited by Daniel Gaido. Winter unknown. Accessed October 1, 2013. http://marxists.org/archive/novack/works/1960/x03.htm.

O, Chris. 2013. Speech Buddies Parents' Corner – Benefits of Early Childhood Education -. August 20. http://www.speechbuddy.com/blog/language-development-2/speech-buddies-parents-corner-benefits-of-early-childhood-education/.

Oleg Atbashian, Larissa Atbashian. 2013. Common Core GED Textbooks: "9/11 hijackers were poor Afghanis". May 11.

Pearson, Inc,. 2013. Parents, Kids and Testing. Unknown Unknown. Accessed November 1, 2013. http://www.parentskidsandtesting.com/#sthash.Vvo0NpO5.dpbs.

Pearson, Inc. 2013. Capacity-Building Support for Your Teaching Effectiveness Initiatives. Unknown Unknown. Accessed October 19, 2013. http://www.pearsonschool.com/index.cfm?locator=PS1sAj.

—. 2013. Pearson 2012 Results. February 25. Accessed September 23, 2013. http://www.pearson.com/news/2013/february/pearson-2012-results.html.

Planned Parenthood. 2012. What is Sex?
http://www.plannedparenthood.org/info-for-teens/sex-
masturbation/what-sex-33828.htm.

Planned Parenthood, The Sex Information and Education
Council of the United States. n.d. "National Sexuality
Education Standards." Future of Sex Ed.
http://www.futureofsexed.org/documents/josh-fose-
standards-web.pdf.

ProQuest. 2012. SIRS Knowledge Source.
http://www.proquestk12.com/productinfo/sirs_knowledges
ource.shtml.

Ravitch, Diane. 2013. David Coleman: The Most
Influential Man in Education? August 31. Accessed
September 11, 2013.
http://dianeravitch.net/2013/08/31/david-coleman-the-
most-influential-man-in-u-s-education/.

—. 2013. James Milgram on the Common Core Standards.
September 11. Accessed September 12, 2013.
http://dianeravitch.net/2013/09/11/james-milgram-on-the-
common-core-math-standards/.

—. 2013. Reign of Error. New York: Alfred A. Knopf.

—. 2010. The Death and Life of the Great American
School System. New York, NY: Basic Books.

Resmovitz, Joyce. 2013. David Coleman, Common Core
Writer, Gears Up for ACT Rewrite. August 30. Accessed
August 30, 2013.
http://www.huffingtonpost.com/2013/08/30/david-
coleman-common-core-sat_n_3818107.html.

Rettner, Rachael. 2011. Are Today's Youth Less Creative
and Imaginative? August 12. Accessed November 2, 2013.
http://www.livescience.com/15535-children-creative.html.

Riede, Paul. 2013. 40 Percent of Syracuse Teachers Need Improvement, Early Evaluation Results Show. October 4. Accessed October 17, 2013. http://www.syracuse.com/news/index.ssf/2013/10/forty_per cent_of_syracuse_teachers_need_improvement_plans_preli minary_evaluation.html#incart_m-rpt-2.

Ritz, Erica. 2013. "Really Spooky" Poem Praising Common Core Allegedly Recited by Dozens of Fifth Graders--Read It Here . August 9. http://www.theblaze.com/stories/2013/08/09/really-spooky-poem-praising-common-core-allegedly-recited-by-dozens-of-5th-graders-at-school-ceremony-read-it-here/.

Roger, Chuck. 2010. Welcome to the Machine: Cultural Marxism in Education. March 31. Accessed October 29, 2013. http://www.americanthinker.com/2010/03/welcome_to_the _machine_cultura.html

Rubenstein, Gary. 2013. My Advice to TFA Staffers: Quit for America. November 15. Accessed November 19, 2013. http://garyrubinstein.teachforus.org/2013/11/15/my-advice-to-tfa-staffers-quit-for-america/.

Sacks, Peter. 1999. Standardized Minds: The High Price of America's Testing Culture and What We Can Do To Change It. New York: Perseus Publishing.

Schlikerman, Becky. 2013. Chicago Teachers Union urges parents to oppose standardized tests for young kids. November 7. Accessed November 7, 2013. ." http://www.suntimes.com/news/metro/23598511-418/chicago-teachers-union-urges-parents-to-oppose-standardized-tests-for-young-kids.html.

Schneider, Mercedes. 2013. A Brief Audit of Bill Gates' Common Core Spending. August 29. Accessed September

4, 2013. http://www.huffingtonpost.com/mercedes-schneider/a-brief-audit-of-bill-gat_b_3837421.html.

—. 2013. Gates Money and Common Core-Part IV. September 19. Accessed September 16, 2013. http://www.huffingtonpost.com/mercedes-schneider/gates-money-and-common-co_2_b_3955641.html.

Schoen, Karen. 2013. Examples of Common Core Propaganda. November 12. http://victoriajackson.com/10039/example-common-core-propaganda.

Schroeder, Karen. 2012. Common Core Standards and the Federalization of Education. October 4. Accessed September 19, 2013. http://conservativeteachersofamerica.com/tag/united-naions/#sthash.cVOxNN5W.dpbs.

Shaw, Anny. 2013. US Government Strengthens Ties with UNESCO. July 12. Accessed October 4, 2013. http://www.theartnewspaper.com/articles/US-government-strengthens-ties-with-Unesco/30101.

Simpson, Mike. 2013. Put to the Test: Adults Sample Common Core. November 9. Accessed November 9, 2013. http://bigeducationape.blogspot.com/2013/11/put-to-test-adults-sample-common-core.html.

Skalicky, Amy. n.d. "Common Core, Girl Scouts, and Pro-Abortion Activism." Elephant Tree Features: Conversations in Boulder County. http://elephanttreefeatures.com/2013/09/19/common-core-the-girl-scouts-and-pro-abortion-activism/.

—. n.d. "Common Core: "Sexuality" Education." Elephant Tree Features: Conversations in Boulder County. http://elephanttreefeatures.com/2013/10/27/common-core-sexuality-education/.

Skills, Partnership for 21st Century. 2002. Partnership for 21st Century Skills. January 1. Accessed October 3, 2013. http://www.p21.org/our-work/p21-framework.

Slekar, Tim. 2012. #optout of #edreform and watch #testing regime implode. December 21. Accessed November 1, 2013. http://atthechalkface.com/2012/12/21/optout-of-edreform-and-watch-testing-regime-implode-2/.

Smith, Frank. 2002. The Glass Wall. New York: Teachers College Press.

Solley, Bobbie. 2007. ACEI Position Paper on Standardized Testing. Fall Unknown. Accessed November 1, 2013. http://www.acei.org/global-action/standardized-testing.html.

SPARK. 2012. Gambling With Our Future, Part 1 and 2: An Alarming Downward Trend in America's Concern for Physical Education. Unknown Unknows. Accessed September 21, 2013. http://www.sparkpe.org/blog/alarming-downward-trend-for-physical-education/.

Steinhagan, Janice. 2013. Common Core "Sea Change" Hits Local Schools. November 11. Accessed November 15, 2013. http://www.remindernews.com/article/2013/11/08/common-core-sea-change-hits-local-schools.

Strauss, Valerie. 2013. 60% of Adults Who Took Standardized Test Bombed. March 19. Accessed October 19, 2013. http://www.washingtonpost.com/blogs/answer-sheet/wp/2013/03/19/sixty-percent-of-adults-who-took-standardized-test-bombed/.

—. 2013. Harvard Student: Don't Teach for America. October 24. Accessed November 2, 2013.

http://www.washingtonpost.com/blogs/answer-sheet/wp/2013/10/24/harvard-student-dont-teach-for-america/.

——. 2013. Pearson Criticized for Finding Test Essay Scorers on Craigslist. January 6. Accessed November 1, 2013. http://www.washingtonpost.com/blogs/answer-sheet/wp/2013/01/16/pearson-criticized-for-finding-test-essay-scorers-on-craigslist/.

——. 2012. The Answer Sheet. January 10. Accessed October 16, 2013. http://www.washingtonpost.com/blogs/answer-sheet/post/ravitch-no-child-left-behind-and-the-damage-done/2012/01/10/gIQAR4gxoP_blog.html.

Strauss, Valeris. 2011. When An Adult Took Standardized Tests Designed for Kids. December 5. Accessed October 13, 2013. http://www.washingtonpost.com/blogs/answer-sheet/post/when-an-adult-took-standardized-tests-forced-on-kids/2011/12/05/gIQApTDuUO_blog.html.

Swanson, Kristen. 2013. Everything You Need to Know About Common Core Testing. July 2. Accessed October 28, 2013. http://thejournal.com/articles/2013/07/02/everything-you-need-to-know-about-common-core-testing.aspx.

Swasey, Christel. 2013. Professor Thomas Newkirk of University of New Hampshire Speaks About Common Core - See more at: http://conservativeteachersofamerica.com/tag/susan-pimentel/#sthash.evtF0Dbr.dpuf. February 18. Accessed September 22, 2013. Professor Thomas Newkirk of University of New Hampshire Speaks About Common Core - See more at: http://conservativeteachersofamerica.com/tag/susan-pimentel/#sthash.evtF0Dbr.dpuf.

—. 2013. Top Ten Scariest People in Education Reform #5-Bill Gates. March 28. Accessed August 3, 2013. http://whatiscommoncore.wordpress.com/2013/03/28/top-ten-scariest-people-in-education-reform-5-bill-gates/.

—. 2013. Top Ten Scariest People in Education Reform #7-Sir Michael Barber. March 23. Accessed November 19, 2013. http://whatiscommoncore.wordpress.com/2013/03/23/top-ten-scariest-people-in-education-reform-7-sir-michael-barber-cea-pearson/.

—. 2013. What's Wrong With Social Justice: Rabbi Lapin Explains. June 6. Accessed October 13, 2013. http://whatiscommoncore.wordpress.com/2013/06/06/whats-wrong-with-social-justice-rabbi-lapin-explains/.

—. 2013. Without Authority: The Federal Access of Private Data Using Common Core. February 24. http://whatiscommoncore.wordpress.com/2013/08/24/without-authority-the-federal-access-of-private-data-using-common-core/.

Swasey, Chrystel. 2013. Top Ten Scariest People in Education Reform: #8 Arne Duncan. March 22. Accessed October 19, 2013. http://whatiscommoncore.wordpress.com/2013/03/22/top-ten-scariest-people-in-education-reform-8-arne-duncan-u-s-secretary-of-education/.

2013. "The United Nations Educational, Scientific and Culteral Organization (UNESCO)." Congressional Research Service. March 18. Accessed October 9, 2013. http://www.fas.org/sgp/crs/row/R42999.pdf.

Thomlinson, Stephen. 2005. "Edward Lee Thorndike and John Dewey on the Science of Education." Western Oregon University. September 14. Accessed September 9, 2013.

http://www.wou.edu/~girodm/611/Thorndike_vs_Dewey.p df.

Thurtell, Craig. 2013. Do the Common Core Standards Flunk History? April 13. Accessed September 18, 2013. http://hnn.us/article/151479.

Tuttle, Erin. 2013. Why Does Common Core Mandate Fuzzy Math? June 10. Accessed October 14, 2013. http://hoosiersagainstcommoncore.com/why-does-common-core-mandate-fuzzy-math/.

UNESCO. 2000. "The Dakar Framework for Action." UNESCO. April 2-3. Accessed September 26, 2013. http://unesdoc.unesco.org/images/0012/001211/121147e.pd f.

—. n.d. "UN's International Guidelines on Sexuality Education." Fox News. http://www.foxnews.com/projects/pdf/082509_unesco.pdf.

UNESCO, Microsoft, Bill Gates. 2004. "Cooperation Agreement Between UNESCO and Microsoft Corporation." Eagle Forum. November 17. Accessed August 27, 2013. http://www.eagleforum.org/links/UNESCO-MS.pdf.

United Nations. 1992. "Agenda 21." Sustainable Development United Nations. June 3. Accessed August 7, 2013. http://sustainabledevelopment.un.org/content/documents/A genda21.pdf.

—. 1992. "United Nations Conference on Environment and Development-Agenda 21." Sustainable Development UN. June 3-14. Accessed September 7, 2013. http://sustainabledevelopment.un.org/content/documents/A genda21.pdf.

Unknown. 2013. About. January 15. Accessed September 7, 2013. http://www.standardswork.org/board.asp.

US Department of Education. 2012. "Family Educational Rights and Privacy Act (FERPA) ." ed.gov. June. http://www2.ed.gov/policy/gen/guid/fpco/pdf/ferpa-disaster-guidance.pdf.

US Dept of Education. 2013. Promoting Grit, Tenacity and Perseverence. February. http://www.ed.gov/edblogs/technology/files/2013/02/OET-Draft-Grit-Report-2-17-13.pdf.

Viteritti, Joseph P. 2013. "The Federal Role in School Reform: Obama's "Race to the Top"." Hunter College: Uran Affairs and Planning. June 12. Accessed October 12, 2013. http://www.hunteruap.org/wp-content/uploads/2012/09/NDLR_Federal-Role-In-School-Reform.pdf.

Westheimer, Joel. 2011. "George S. Counts (1889–1974) - Sociology and Education, Social Reform, Political Activism, Contribution." Education University State University.com. Unknown Unknown. Accessed October 4, 2013. http://education.stateuniversity.com/pages/1891/Counts-George-S-1889-1974.html.

William Klemm, D.V.M., Ph.D. 2013. What Learning Cursive Does for Your Brain. March 14. Accessed October 18, 2013. http://www.psychologytoday.com/blog/memory-medic/201303/what-learning-cursive-does-your-brain.

Yurica, Katharine. 2004. Conquering by Stealth and Deception. September 14. Accessed August 13, 2013. http://www.yuricareport.com/Dominionism/TheSwiftAdvanceOfaPlannedCoup.htm.

Yurica, Katherine. 2004. Conquering by Stealth and Deception. September 14. Accessed August 13, 2013. http://www.theocracywatch.org/yurica_weyrich_manual.htm.

Made in the USA
San Bernardino, CA
27 August 2014